What Readers Say About

Numidia books

"Congratulations on *Bridges, Routers, Gateways!* This book is a techno-simple **marvel**! I use it to train the network analysts who report to me, and the info also fits well into the Network Analysis class I teach at UCLA Extension.

Chuck Hollins, Network Manager, Los Angeles County

"**All your books are great**, but I especially like *Routers!* because of the spiral binding. It lies flat, for easier access... "

- Robert LaPosta, network engineer

"[The] **highly readable style** [of *LANs!*] was enjoyable and the insights informative…Keep up the good work of addressing an often misunderstood arena of communications technology."

—Harrell Van Norman, consultant/author

"Keep writing your books. *Bridges, Routers!* was very well written, to the point, and comprehensive. It makes an **excellent reference guide**.

- CNA & MCSE-certified network analyst, Cedars-Sinai Medical Center

"**Well-done**, almost effortless learning, written simply, light of jargon, with **terms clearly defined** as they come up. The information is all there, most often graphically depicted. It is also **instructionally sound**—it starts with review of the basics and gradually builds new information on what has already been clearly presented."

—Rita Lewis, Instructional Designer

Reviewers Agree!

"An **exceptionally good** study guide that will enable the earnest student to firmly grasp the complexities of LAN internetworking. Upon completion of this series, the network manager should be able to cut through vendor hoopla and cull the most salient information necessary to successfully build a corporate internetwork."

—Maureen Molloy, Network World

LANs! "...**communicates concepts extremely well**. Takes a **real-world**, hands-on approach." **Rated A** (= excellent)

—Computer Book Review

"Now there's a middle ground [between live training and consultants]: a self learning guide that **allows net managers to go at their own pace** and ask questions about their networks along the way.... The exams at the end of each chapter take some unusual forms, from internetwork design projects to crossword puzzles."

—Data Communications Magazine

Mastering Gigabit Ethernet, ATM & Other High-Speed LANs

Self-Paced Learning Series

V.C. Marney-Petix and Sandrella Salins

Numidia Press
Fremont, CA 94536

Mastering Gigabit Ethernet, ATM & Other High-Speed LANs

Self-Paced Learning Series

Printed in the United States of America.

Library of Congress CIP block in progress

Why This Book?

(Read me!)

This book, and its associated course in the Marpet University curriculum, is a detailed look at Gigabit Ethernet, Asynchronous Transfer Mode (ATM), switching, Fast Ethernet and related technologies, designed for network managers, administrators, chief financial officers, technical support reps, sales and marketing professionals and others who want to understand options prior to making a very expensive decision. When we mention expense, we are not referring to purchase costs. In general, the on-going operations costs, not to mention training, re-training and bad morale attendant on a bad decision almost always far outweigh the mere purchase costs. In this realm it is especially important to make the right decision.

It is a major theme of this book that there is NO SINGLE CORRECT ANSWER TO THIS QUESTION of Gigabit Ethernet vs. ATM and other technologies. There is a correct answer for your network. There is probably a different correct answer for someone else's. For darn sure, you won't make a reasoned, long-term good decision by choosing whatever the technical media (bless their hearts) is over-hyping this year.

Acknowledgments

As always, my (VM) appreciation goes first to the attendees at my various Marpet University, public and onsite classes and seminars and University Extension classes, here in the USA and in Mexico, Colombia, New Zealand, etc. I love to explore the differences in our national needs as I enjoy the similarities. (Dumb decisions are a remarkably universal human inclination.) These devoted learners ask the tough questions that even my consulting clients forget to ask, forcing me to think more deeply about many issues.

As far as information sources are concerned, I (still VM) dutifully consulted the Web pages of all the GE and ATM vendors before sending this manuscript to the technical reviewers. Getting those technical reviewers was a story of stealth and derring-do, that I unfortunately cannot recount full details of. Suffice it to say that too many vendors use "go look at our Web page" to get out of actually having to support their customers after the sale. When it comes to really getting the straight information, I need to ask real people detailed questions. (I also have tendinitis and carpal tunnel damage, so writing long detailed email queries is not possible. I have to talk.) As a result of my extensive talking, the technical reviewers didn't hate the original mss. too much, we had very little rewrite to do and the book has gone to press only 3 months behind schedule.

We want to especially thank Dirk Campbell of 3Com, Bernard Daines, estimable CEO of Packet Engines Inc. and Roy Ng, even more estimable ATM consultant of Toronto, Canada, for their extra-special effort.

It appears that one of us (we won't admit who) has been driving the fine copyeditors of Numidia Press crazy with a plethora of allegedly gratuitous parentheses. It's not so! We need every single one of the little darlings. We appreciate the expertise and saintly patience of the Numidia staff, especially during the production phase of this book. As far as the collaboration is concerned: all the good stuff is Sandrella's fault; all the mistakes are Victoria's.

Dedication

To my devoted furry family: Charlie, Beth, Chester, Brianna, Lizzie and Jane (the bunnies) and Chulalongkorn, Gabriel, Gayle and Arthur Wellington (the cats). Thanks to you, I'm still sane.

To Ellen Brigham, a better friend that I will ever deserve if I live to be 200, who keeps asking me tough business questions, making wise business suggestions and telling me it's OK to eat chocolate.

To Joan Simien, a shining light in the spiritual darkness.

With gratitude, to the memory of Hannibal of Carthage, a patriot who battled corruption and special privilege because it was The Right Thing to Do, even though he lost the election and was driven into exile and death as a consequence. May we be inspired to do as well in this century.

And finally, to my co-author, another sister-of-my-heart, who believes in me when no sensible person would. I can finally tell you how much I appreciate all you've done for me. (VM)

I (SS) am indebted to many warm and wonderful people whose personal bravery has been endless. However, I will focus on my inner circle.

To my daughter. Sandrella Jr., who is now entering young adulthood and each day helps me to uncover aspects of my youth that I had not known were unexplored. She is my peace.

To my son, Winter, who is so young, fearless and noble. Thank you for being the fire in my life.

To Bernard who has laughed and cried at this world with me for many years. It is "we."

To my life-long friend and business partner, Victoria. I am so blessed to know you.

Table of Contents

0
LAN Basics Review

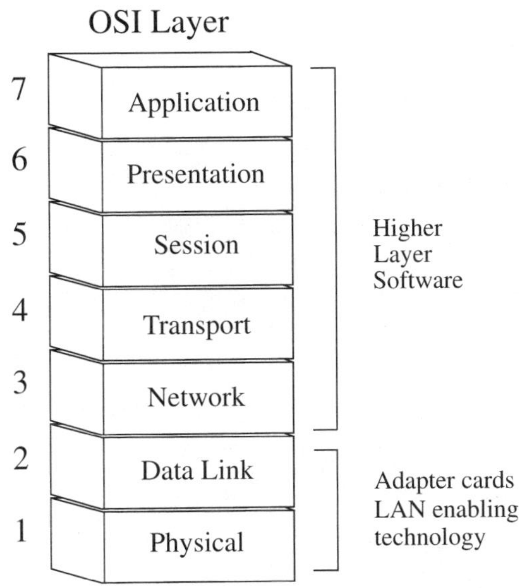

Do please read this chapter, regardless of your incoming skill level - so that you can warm up your brain for the exercise to come and review key concepts of the 2 most important networking models and the most important network protocol stack.

IEEE Model

The IEEE developed a 2 layer model for the basic network functions that Ethernet, Token Ring, FDDI and ATM perform in the network, so let's review the basic functions and their layers.

The Physical Layer translates the 1s and 0s that your computer, codec, etc. uses internally into 1s and 0s that are coded in the way that ATM needs. Each specific medium within each technology requires a different **line code**. The line code specifies the specific electrical voltage or light/dark changes that mean a "1" or a "0." This Layer also defines the shape and size of plugs, connectors, adapters, the size and type of the wires, fiber or airwaves that may be used and other "physical" things.

The Data Link Layer of a network defines software as well as hardware. Here we assign each device a specific local address (usually on an adapter card), we define an access method (contention and token-passing in traditional networks) and we detect bit errors (usually the field at the very end of the frame). All these functions are actually included in the MAC sublayer of the Data Link Layer.

The OSI Model's 7 layers cover all the functions in a LAN, including all the software above the Data Link Layer.

The Data Link & Network Addresses

Let's discuss what we mean when we say "the network." To be precise, a network is composed of traffic sources and destinations - endstations - and the devices that never act as endpoints of a transmission. Endstations can be desktops, printers/plotters, servers, and related devices. The network infrastructure, that carries traffic but doesn't originate it, includes routers, bridges, switches, hubs, wires, WAN access devices and related devices. When we are talking about the network in this book's discussion of ATM, keep this definition of "the network" in mind and visualize routers, switches and bridges (including WAN access devices). Also keep in mind that: 1) most "routers" today include switches (and see 3) and one or more gateways inside them, 2) WAN access devices include routers and gateways, 3) switches include bridge software and so on.

The **Network Layer**'s job is to connect a network to another network - which is also the router job. The Network Layer header specifies a network address and other parameters that routers use to get the frame to its ultimate destination. The **network address** specifies the ultimate sender and receiver. IP and IPX addresses are Network Layer addresses. Bear in mind that a Data Link address always specifies the immediate destination of a frame on the local LAN. So when an endstation is preparing a frame for the network and it looks at the network layer addresses and sees that the destination is on another network, it will NOT put the ultimate destination's MAC address in the MAC destination field. It puts the local router's address there, right?

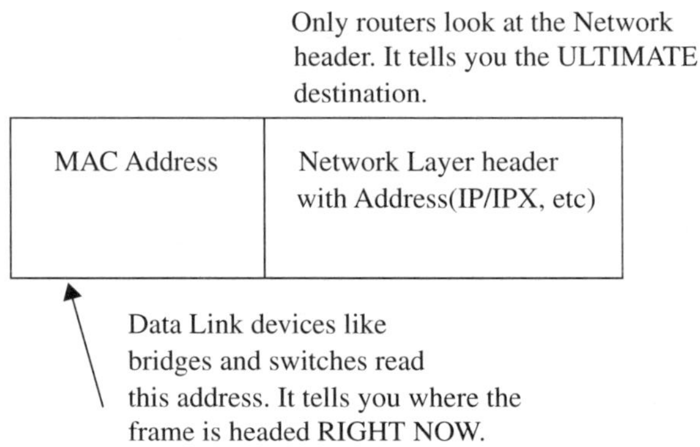

Datagrams & IP

In legacy networks, routers route IP and IPX, which are **datagram (connectionless)** protocols. Each packet is separately routed along what seems to be the fastest route available at the moment the packet arrives at the router.

For network management, credit card verification networks and other transaction-oriented networks, all you need is to get one individual packet to its destination. For most other applications, you have a stream of packets that together make up a file download, an email message or anything else bigger than one payload.

So the IP datagram process of looking at each packet individually means that individual packets in the stream could end up taking different paths through the network and could arrive out of order at the destination. If a packet gets lost from the middle of a message or file, you would also like to know that.

You need an additional protocol to ensure end-to-end reception of the entire file, a protocol that will re-order the misordered packets and require retransmission of the little lost lambs. What you use in IP networks is TCP, a virtual circuit, connection-oriented protocol we will review next.

Datagram protocols allow you to multicast and broadcast. Broadcast addresses mean "everyone." Broadcast is a special case of the more generic multicast address, which means "member of a group." Routers talk to each other using the all-routers multicast MAC address, for example. Bridges discuss spanning trees using the all-bridges multicast MAC address. The MAC protocol (Ethernet, FDDI, ATM, etc.) reserves specific addresses for all-routers and all-bridges multicasts.

The Internet Protocol Suite

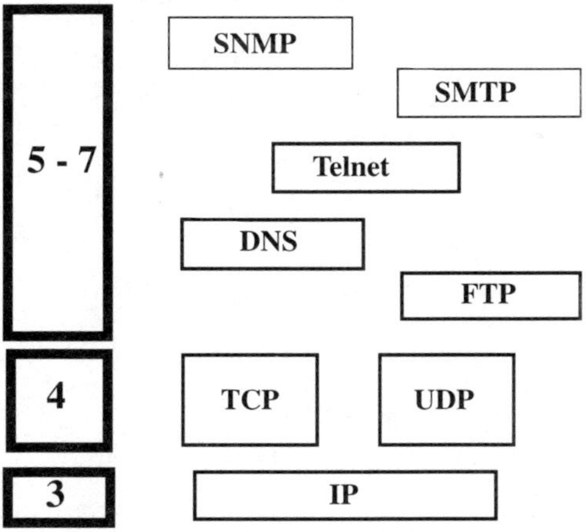

Below IP, you must have a network access technology like Ethernet, Token Ring, FDDI or ATM.

Virtual Circuits

To understand virtual circuits, consider a telephone call. When you dial a number, the telephone network sends a connection setup packet to the destination number you requested. The network alerts the destination by creating a "ringing" sound. Along the way, the setup packet went through switches that looked at the destination address and allocated bandwidth for the call that was going to start. The call was allocated a 64 Kbps channel, of course, known as a DS-0 pipe. This telephony example allocated an actual physical channel for the call.

In the data network world, we don't pre-allocate physical bandwidth for a particular sender and receiver to exchange packets. What we do is create **virtual circuits** (VCs). We can do this in one of two ways: 1) by involving only the sender and receiver in knowing about the VC (what TCP does), so the network can send the individual pieces of the message through different switches/routers, or 2) by setting up a specific physical path that the VC has to take (as ATM and Frame Relay do).

In this second case, the routers and switches along the way have tables of VC#s, telling them where specific VCs have to go - in one port and out another. As they move through the switch, their virtual circuit #s change. The switch knows that packets with VC# 3 coming in on port 2 must be sent out port 4 with a new VC # of 6. This process is known as **label swapping** and it is much faster than consulting a routing table or even examining a long sender and receiver address.

In packets using TCP and IP, after the IP header you have a TCP header that includes fields to assign the same VC numbers to all the packets associated with a particular message, acknowledgment numbers that allow the receiver to indicate that a particular packet was received and sequence numbers that allow the receiver to put the incoming packets that belong to a VC into proper order so that the message gets reassembled properly.

A common application for datagram service at both the Network and Transport Layer is a credit card verification (point-of-sale, POS) network. When the store clerk runs a credit card through a machine, it creates a single packet for delivery to a distant database. A single packet returns with a yes or no answer. If a packet gets lost, the clerk will eventually run the card through again. This kind of network uses UDP instead of TCP.

It is rare for an entire network to be designed with only one option at the Transport Layer, as the POS network is. In most cases, the network designers allow the traffic creators (workstations, servers, mainframes, etc.) the option of creating a packet from either UDP or TCP. This means that each application will choose one of the protocols at this layer, depending of which is appropriate. The only applications that use UDP are network operations and management. The SNMP protocol, used in IP networks, runs on UDP, for example. If the traffic source is a network management station, it will create an SNMP query that is only one packet long; the answer from the managed device ("I'm fine, thanks for asking.") will also fit into a single payload. This means that all network management queries will be messages that are no more than 1 packet in length. If the entire message can be carried in a single packet, you have no need to put pieces back together in order and you have no need of virtual circuits.

Virtual circuit service, without a fixed path like TCP or with a fixed path like ATM and Frame Relay, is known as connection-oriented service, because you are setting up a virtual connection between sender and receiver. With a fixed path VC, you can visualize a pipe connecting two network users. You can see how this protects packets from ever getting out of order. You can also see that this connection does NOT easily lend itself to multicast or broadcast concepts.

Terminology Note: A router looks at the Network Layer header, so we say that a router handles **packets**. A packet is part of the frame - the part that starts with the Network Layer header and includes all the other headers, plus the payload. If you take a packet and add the Data Link Layer header to it, you have a frame. The only entity that has any "real" existence is a frame; frames are what actually move from place to place in the network.

The only time that the NIC will put the ultimate destination's MAC address in the MAC destination field is when the ultimate destination is actually on the same network (has the same network number) as the sender. "Foreign" addresses at the Network Layer mean "send this frame to the router, you can't get this frame to the destination with a MAC address."

Desktops must be told the MAC address of their local router (aka default gateway), either manually or via the server at IP address assignment time.

Routing and Switching

Routers act as firewalls in your network because they isolate each of their ports (technically, a network), and don't allow broadcast storms to proliferate. That is why you need to send "foreign" addresses to the router, so it can act as a wall for the traffic you don't want to go everywhere. The router looks at the IP address to decide the ultimate destination of the frame.

There has been a lot of press on the subject of replacing routers with Layer 3 switches, IP switches and the like to "make the network faster." You may purchase products that run faster than your current products, but please be aware that anything that looks at the IP address or functions at the IP layer is technically a router. Period.

In Chapter 2 of this book, you will have an opportunity to expand your understanding of LAN switching. The development of LAN switching is a Layer 2 phenomenon that has had nothing but effects in the local network. We now can give up our Physical Layer hubs (which are multiport repeaters) and put MAC/Data Link switches (which are multiport bridges) close to the users. This is very powerful and exciting - and, of course, introduces a plethora of new, annoying technical problems in some networks. But that's the subject of another discussion!

Now you're all warmed up and ready for High-Speed Networks.

1
Your LAN Infrastructure

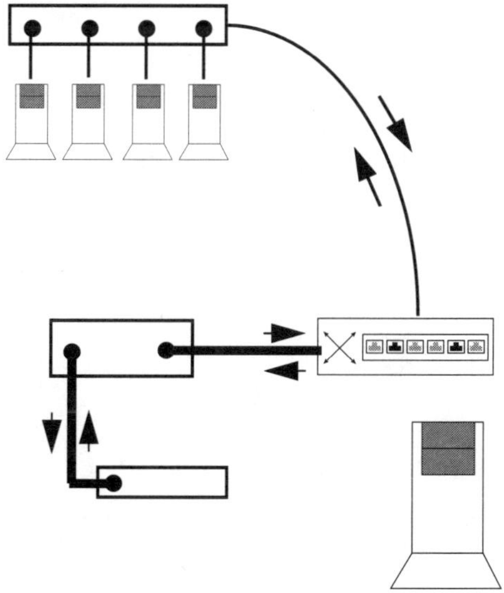

Goals of this Chapter

When you complete this chapter, you should be able to:

- ❐ Discuss the roles and needs of a backbone
- ❐ Develop a list of your backbone needs
- ❐ Determine what needs could be served by a new technology

What is a backbone?

A backbone is:

a) the LAN segments that connect the workgroup segments together, but which don't have direct user connections on them

b) the vertical wiring

c) the most important part of the network infrastructure

d) the part of the network that ATM and Gigabit Ethernet are fighting over today.

All of these definitions are true.

The backbone should be a ring, mesh or full-duplex bus that connects concentrators or switches (which may or may not have routers incorporated in them). From these backbone concentrators, you will connect intermediate or workgroup switches in a star pattern. Some technologists call these trees instead of stars. Your servers should be gathered into **server farms** and put on their own switch. You might give these servers special consideration for a high-speed upgrade. As you examine your network traffic patterns, you will clearly see that between 60-80% of your backbone traffic is destined for your servers. Putting the servers together allows you to give them the bandwidth upgrades and other implementation "special considerations" they need.

By clearing user devices and other direct traffic generators (servers, for example) from part of the network infrastructure, you create a more manageable backbone for your network.

A backbone should connect star-wired hubs, switches and routers only

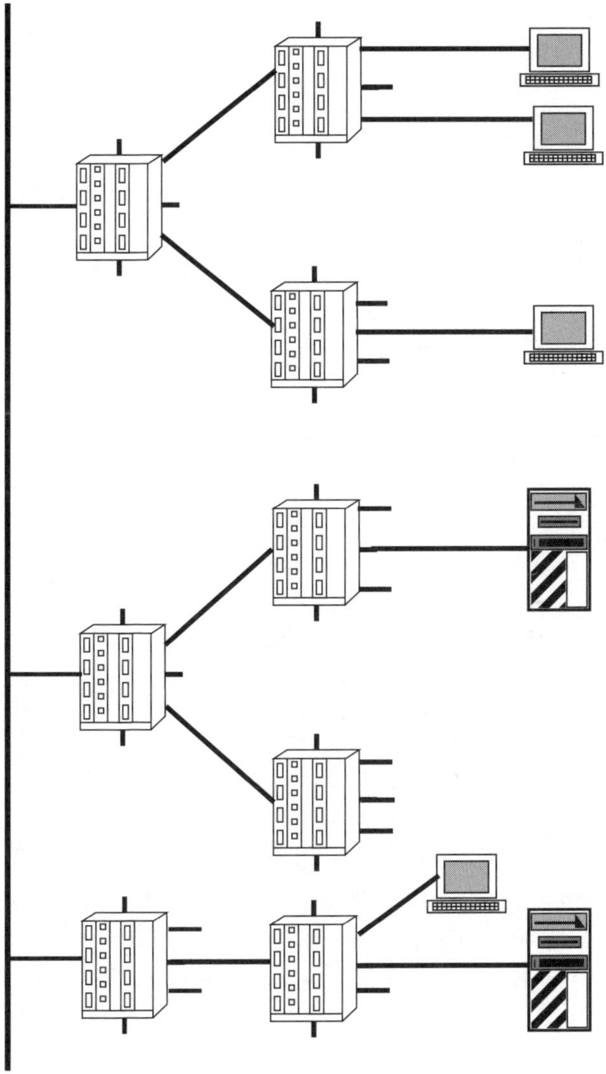

Evolution of Traffic on the Backbone

As late as the early 90s, many organizations did not have a well-formulated backbone implementation or backbone plan. Then several things happened:

- client/server networking became popular and
- people starting actually using multimedia (voice and video) over their networks.

Both these changes added traffic to the network. The first bullet changed the LAN traffic mix from 80% local and 20% backbone to 80% backbone and 20% local - because client/server networking assumes you have global server farms attached to switches that are attached to your backbone!

The net result of these 2 trends (and others) is that the amount of traffic traversing the average large organizational backbone is skyrocketing. As the traffic increases and as we increasingly put our organizationally-critical applications on the network, the role of the backbone in the overall network design becomes of overwhelming importance.

Network managers consider putting high-speed LAN technologies in the parts of the network that most need it, naturally. That means that the backbone is the place where traditional technologies come to their Waterloo. The backbone and the server farm are the first places we need to look, when we consider the high-speed network types in this book. And the backbone and the server farm are the first places you will consider when you tote up your high-speed needs.

Let's start.

Client/Server Networking

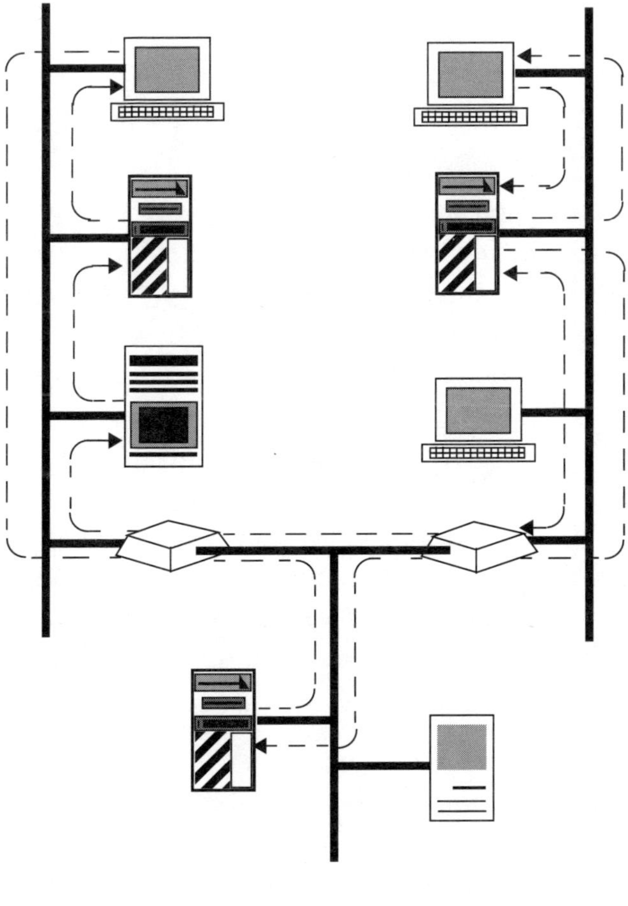

Common Backbone Technologies

Backbones today are primarily:

- FDDI, using MM-PMD (multi-mode fiber)
- Token Ring (16 Mbps)
- Fast Ethernet (100base-TX)

About 10% of backbones are ATM and 12% are other technologies, mostly proprietary products.

There is a common denominator in these choices - speed. We choose a backbone technology because that is the portion of our network where we require the greatest bandwidth. The fact that ATM is available with a Physical Layer of 622 Mbps has been an important part of its appeal; we have the lure of a long-term solution to our bandwidth needs. However, the recent development of Gigabit Ethernet means we now have 2 choices for the more-than-200 Mbps network segment. The other choice we frequently make is the choice of a backbone that can carry videoconferencing. ATM was certainly designed for that - but as you will see in Chapter 3, Gigabit Ethernet may be able to work as well for you.

Before we plunge into technologies, let's start with the needs of your specific network.

If your backbone doesn't look like the illustrations in this chapter and you can see some ways to move devices, put servers into farms or group technology types together so less translation is needed, please incorporate that information into the next project we are going to do.

Backbones

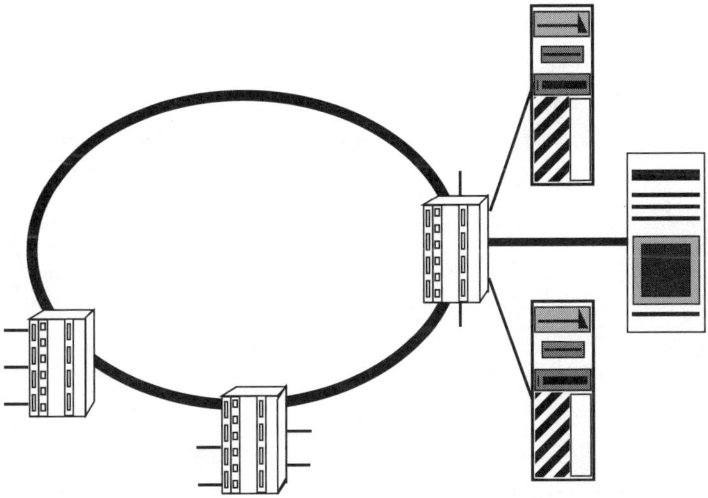

Backbone Needs

1). You should have network topology maps that tell you:

- what devices are where

Get them out, make a copy and let's get to work on the rest of the information you need to plan a backbone upgrade.

2) You also need to know the following for your workgroups:

- traffic levels
- traffic types
- variation in traffic levels through the day/week/month/year
- projected growth in traffic level and changes in types through the next 3 years (if you go beyond 3 years, your prediction accuracy drops to Way Off, so don't bother)

3) When you have plotted these numbers on your maps, you can see some worst-case scenarios for what your workgroups will be pouring into your backbone(s). This will take some time. Don't stint.

4.) Plot the pathways that carry the most critical traffic. You can use colored pencils as an overlay.

5.) Plot the pathways that include translations. Don't just circle the translators (gateways that may be inside the switches & routers as well as standalone devices.). Look at the entire path from the sender to the receiver. If you make changes to the translation points you need this end-to-end understanding.

6). Plot the traffic or application pathways that cause the most complaints. These may be the same as the key applications, or the paths with the translations.

Summary 1-6: Now you can see some areas where you are, or soon will be, in trouble, or you can see some areas where you would like to improve service to the end users.

7). If you have a poor backbone design, now is the time to incorporate ideas into the new plan. (General ideas for improving backbones are also included in the Network Management and Router books in this series.)

8.) On a separate page, or on the same plan if you have space, note the workgroups that are planning videoconferencing or any other application that needs live, realtime voice or video. (Stored video and voice, as we'll discuss later in the ATM chapters, requires lots of bandwidth but not end-to-end jitter control, so ignore it.)

9). Trace out the entire path that the traffic will take across the network. Can you get this traffic onto its own, non-backbone path? If not, you will need to accommodate this isochronous traffic in your backbone plan. Your backbone design must include a technology that can accommodate isochronous traffic or is so bandwidth-rich that congestion will never (well, hardly ever) be a problem.

10.) Look at the translated traffic. Could you eliminate some of these translations by migrating some Data Link technologies from workgroups and standardizing on a smaller (ideally 2 or less) number of technologies? The smaller the number of translations, the less complex the network will be and the lower your operations costs will be. If you cannot get rid of some of these technologies and translations, this information has to be incorporated into your backbone plan. You have our profoundest sympathies. (You are not alone, especially if the reason the technology cannot be abandoned is essentially political, i.e. Bob is the VP of Network Stuff and Bob loves IBM. Period.)

11). Look at the data path that comprises the most problem or complaint-heavy sections of the network. Are users essentially needing more bandwidth to solve their problems? If so, good, because you are preparing to solve that problem. If not, perhaps you can get rid of some of the technologies, equipment, etc. that are causing trouble and lowering overall network efficiency as part of the high-speed revamp. Remember, if a particular device, technology, etc. is sapping your network management staff's time and energy, those are real $$ you are wasting on a daily basis.

You also have to keep in mind that choosing a brand-new technology type for a network upgrade can make your network more problem prone than it already is. A brand-new technology tends to include products that are barely working and only marginally functional; we all make jokes about buying beta-test products labelled as ready for prime-time. (Vendors don't want to hear that. Too bad.) If your major reason for wanting an upgrade is to reduce the litany of complaints and outages, don't choose a technology that is barely birthed. You will not achieve your goal of a peaceful life.

Summary: 7-11: You now know that you require a solution with a certain available bandwidth, with a certain tolerance for isochronous traffic, with a certain tolerance for exotic translations and other specific aspects of your network.

You are now ready to apply your criteria to the technical choices for upgrades that exist in the world today. The purpose of this exercise is to get you to think carefully about what **YOU** need in **your** network. Until you accomplish this labor-intensive task, you are not prepared to launch yourself into fact-finding on technologies. A rather "boring" un-sexy switching upgrade might serve you well; you might need a full-scale makeover to ATM or Gigabit Ethernet; you might need any one of a hundred other solutions. You won't know what's right for you until you have numbers.

Lord Kelvin said (translated from the British), "If you don't have numbers, you don't really know what you're talking about." While demonstrably untrue in human interpersonal relations, his words are very important for network managers to keep in mind. We **do** need numbers to understand what our networks need.

2
Switching

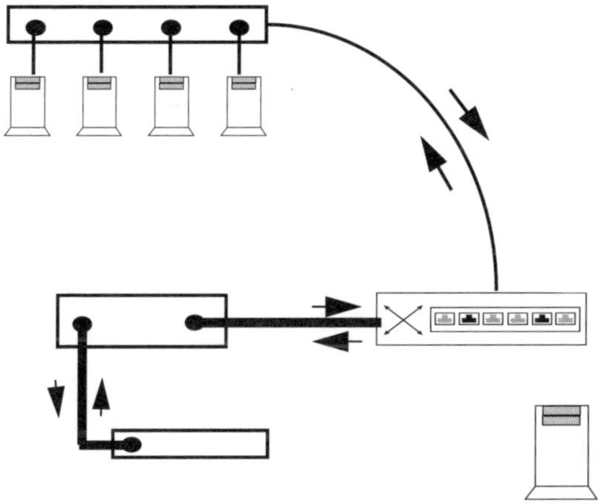

Goals of this Chapter

When you complete this chapter, you should be able to:

- ❐ Define switch, and describe a switch's function in a network
- ❐ Explain switch operation in Ethernet, comparing it to bridge and hub operations
- ❐ List 4 types of switches and explain the best uses for each type
- ❐ Make recommendations for switch placement in the network, citing standards, types and options.

Replacing Hubs With Switches

Before we consider new technologies, let's take a look at a new product type that allows you to conserve as much of your existing infrastructure as possible - the **switch**.

In this chapter, we will look at

- what switches are
- kinds of switches
- making the switching decision.

Let us start by saying that a switch is a fundamental infrastructure connectivity device that replaces hubs. You understand what hubs are for - Physical Layer connectivity. A **hub** is a multi-port **repeater**. Let's review what it is that a hub does, and the types of repeaters that we already have in the network.

A repeater looks at each bit and decides if it is a 1 or a 0, then regenerates a perfect bit. This is a simple Layer 1 function. Buffered repeaters hold a string of bits (usually a frame) in the buffer until the entire frame is received then regenerate all the bits on the outgoing port(s). This is an advantage, since you don't want to waste network resources proliferating frame fragments and other detritus. The 802.3 committee defined 2 different kinds of repeaters when they were defining Fast Ethernet in the "u" subcommittee.

Hubs Incorporate Repeaters

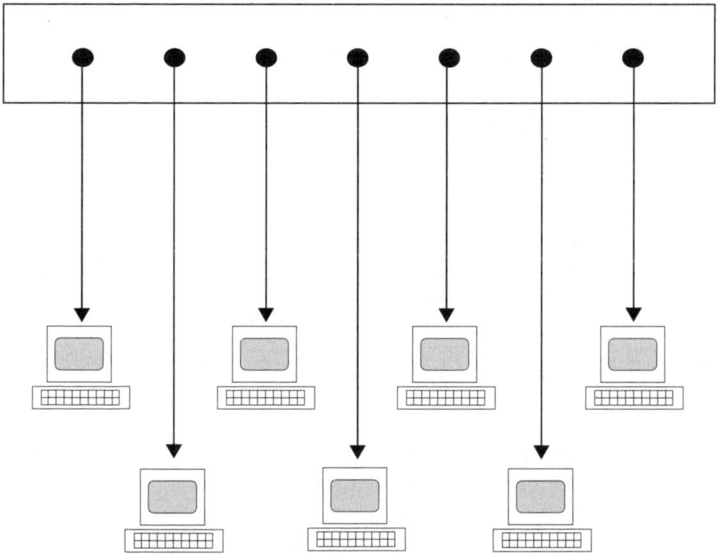

All these devices share bandwidth

Hubs and Switches

Repeaters are classified as **Class I** or **Class II** (sometimes **Type I/II**). A Class I repeater is not stackable; a Class II is. Class I repeaters also cannot be daisy-chained. You must have a Layer 2 or Layer 3 device (bridge, switch or router) between Class I repeaters in the network. Class II repeaters are the devices that allow cable distances listed in the standards (100 meters for Cat. 5 cable, for example). Class I repeaters can only support runs of half the cited distance for each medium.

Most of the hubs in your network are probably stackable and/or daisy-chainable, so they are Class II repeaters, right? A Class II repeater is as sophisticated as a Physical Layer device can get. To get more intelligent, you have to move up to the Data Link Layer and become a bridge.

Let's review how an Ethernet hub propagates frames. First of all, can it read the Ethernet destination address and send the frame to the correct destination port?

Of course not! This is a Physical Layer device; it doesn't read Data Link/MAC addresses. All it can do is pull the entire frame into a buffer, make sure the FCS is correct, then propagate (copy) the frame on ALL the available ports, including the backbone port. If your "intelligent" hub reads addresses, it's a bridge, regardless of what the vendor's Marketing Department thinks sounds "cool" this year. The other critical issue in hub function is that all the devices on the hub are sharing the bandwidth. If it is a 10 Mbps hub, you are all sharing 10 Mbps. If it is a 100 Mbps hub, you have more to share, but you are still sharing.

What is a Switch?

A workgroup switch has the same place in the network as a hub: you put it in workgroups to replace hubs. With a fundamental difference, of course. Basically, switches are for people and devices who hate to share.

Each port on the switch is a private LAN segment for the devices connected to the port. The advantage of using a switch in place of a hub is that each of the attached devices has its own 10 Mbps "data pipe" into the switch. Hubs require devices to share the same 10 Mbps, so if one device is talking, the others must wait and collisions are possible. (It's not the actual collisions that cause problems, but the interframe latencies that we have to build into the contention mechanism to prevent collisions and to ensure fair access that slow things down.)

In an Ethernet switch, each port is a separate **collision domain**. (That means that you can only collide with people on your port.) If each port is connected to only one NIC, then you cannot have collisions unless the switch is trying to send you a frame at the exact same millisecond that you are trying to send a frame to the switch; this is a rare event, as the distances are very short. In the illustration, you can see a workgroup switch with a desktop PC, a printer and a server. Each port is connected to only one device (NIC).

To be more technical: a switch is a multi-port **bridge** with dedicated port-port connections.

The Switching Fabric

The switch has one additional technical difference from both hubs and bridges and that is the way that frames are transferred from port to port within the device.

In both hubs and bridges, we depend on a **backplane**, which is a shared, very fast internal transfer medium. A switch tries to prevent contention within the device, and speed port-to-port transfer, by allocating the backplane bandwidth into pre-assigned logical channels. The transfer between port 1 and port 2 has a specific channel, the transfer between port 5 and port 8 has a different channel and so on for all the possible bi-directional combinations for all the ports on the device.

The port-to-port transfer across the specific channels, instead of across a shared backplane, is the essence of switching. The phrase **switching fabric** has become popular lately. Sometimes the entire collection of switches in the network are referred to as one big switching fabric.

Because a switch looks at the MAC address of every frame, it can perform **address isolation** - that is, making sure that the only frames that come down the wire from a switch port are frames that are actually addressed to that port, or are broadcast/multicast frames.

Because it is a MAC device, switches cannot stop broadcast storms. If you network is entirely composed of switches, you have the equivalent of a router-less bridged network - not a clever idea.

Switches

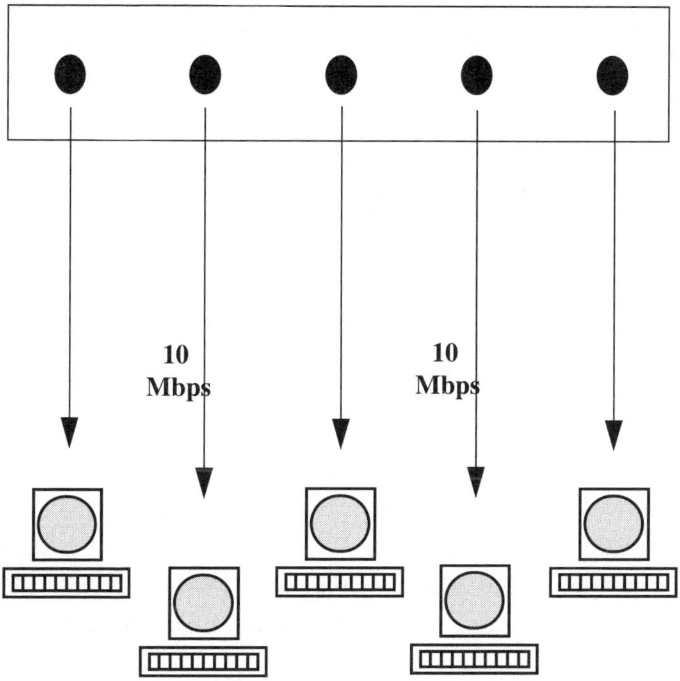

Address Isolation

The switch creates a port table (similar in function to a bridge's address table), matching addresses to each port. As a device comes "alive" on the network, it sends out a frame and the switch discovers who is attached to it.

A switch will cut down on inter-port traffic compared to using a hub because traffic that is not destined for a locally-known address will be shipped out on the backbone port(s) - upstream - and any downstream daisy-chained ports. (A stacked hub or stacked switch acts as one entity to the rest of the network, but it will know to send frames to its stacked partners in this context.)

The frames that travel to other switches, hubs, bridges or routers will then be acted on by those devices, as they feel they should. Whereas a hub will copy the frame to all ports, the bridge or switch will perform a port address check. These devices will forward only to the specific destination port if the destination address is local or to the backbone if it is not.

The router, with supreme insouciance, will ignore all frames that are not addressed to it personally - except to update its local addresses list for last-hop routing. In extreme cases, if certain devices communicate only locally and never are seen by the local router, they will not show up in the local addresses database and cannot be contacted from outside the network. Some vendors allow switches to ship their address tables upstream to the router. (Confused about routers? Check out the router book in this series.)

Address Isolation

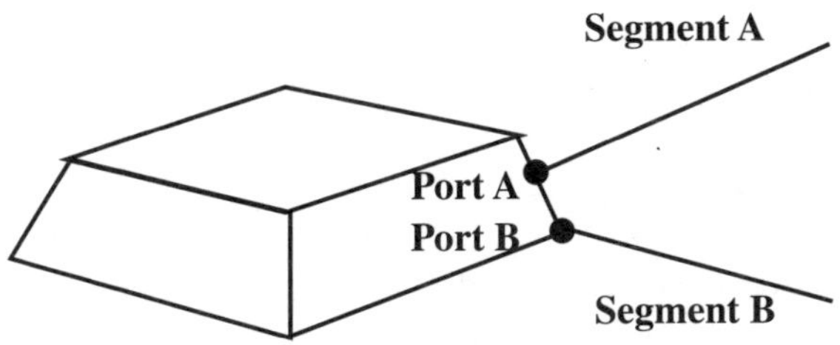

Segment A	Segment B
29	16

Because a switch is a bridge, you should make sure your vendor follows the Spanning Tree (transparent bridging) standard. If it uses a proprietary protocol for switch-switch communication to prevent Data Link loops, you are locked into a single-vendor network!

The term **downstream** means "toward the users" and **upstream** means "toward the backbone." If your topologies are stars, this will be very easy to see in your network maps.

Types of Switches

There are 3 basic architectures for Data Link switches:

• **cut-through,** which have (thankfully) lost their allure in the market and have evolved into

• **modified cut-through**

• **store-and-forward**

A store-and-forward switch acts just like a bridge. It copies the entire frame into the buffer, so that it can check the FCS for bit errors before forwarding it.

A cut-through switch begins forwarding the frame onto the destination port or the backbone port(s) as soon as it reads the destination MAC address. This means that frames with bit errors and illegally long or short frames will be propagated onto the network. This wastes bandwidth, of course, since these frames will just be thrown out prior to delivery.

The modified cut-through switch waits until it gets at least a minimum-length frame before it begins to cut-through to the destination port. Most cut-through switch models have evolved into modified cut-throughs.

You should never attach a cut-through or modified cut-through switch to a backbone. Recent studies have shown a less than 6 millisecond difference in performance between store-and-forward and the other switch types. There being no appreciable advantage to even modified cut-through, we recommend you buy only store-and-forward switches.

Types of Switches

Cut Thru

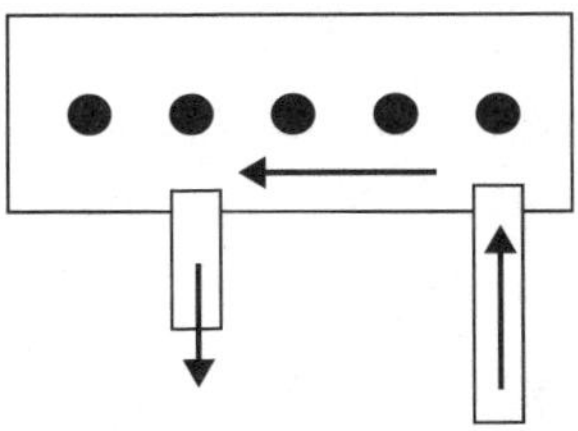

• Forwarding as soon as address is read

Store-and-Forward

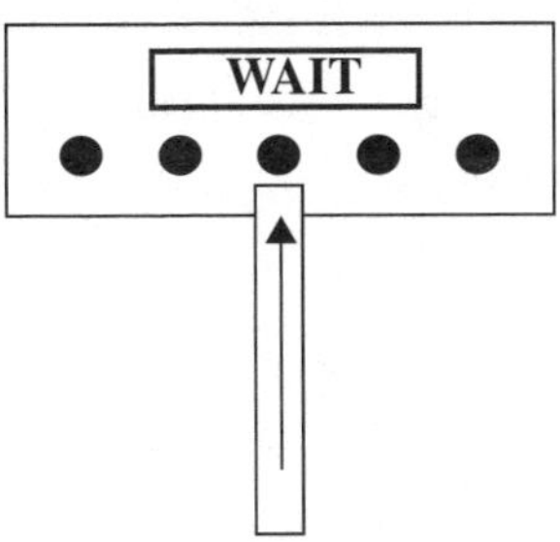

• No forwarding until the frame is checked

A switch that connects to the backbone, with no user connection, is called an **enterprise switch**.

Using Switches

The final type of switch is a **full-duplex** switch. On a full-duplex Ethernet switch, every port delivers 10 Mbps in each direction. If it is a backbone connection between 2 switches, you can imagine 10 Mbps moving left to right while another 10 Mbps moves right to left. You need no additional wire; 2 pairs of Cat 5 UTP can carry full-duplex. Full-duplex switching is a particularly good upgrade solution for backbones, giving you dedicated switch-to-switch connections.

You will deploy your switches as you have deployed your hubs - in trees radiating from a backbone out to the users (the leaves, if you will).

If you put your servers in a server farm on the backbone, and attach the server farm to the backbone with a backbone switch, you will probably boost your backbone traffic. In fact, studies have shown that client/sever implementations typically put 80% of the available traffic onto the backbone, heading to or from those global servers.

We recommend that you consider switching as a way to boost bandwidth to connected devices before you consider migrating to an entirely new technology. In general, the upgrade costs and the associated costs (training of entire staff, etc.) are lower if your new infrastructure is a switched version of whatever frame type you used to use. On the other hand, you have to make sure you do not underestimate the differences associated with moving to switching, as we will explore in the next chapter as we explore faster Ethernet versions.

Full-Duplex Switches

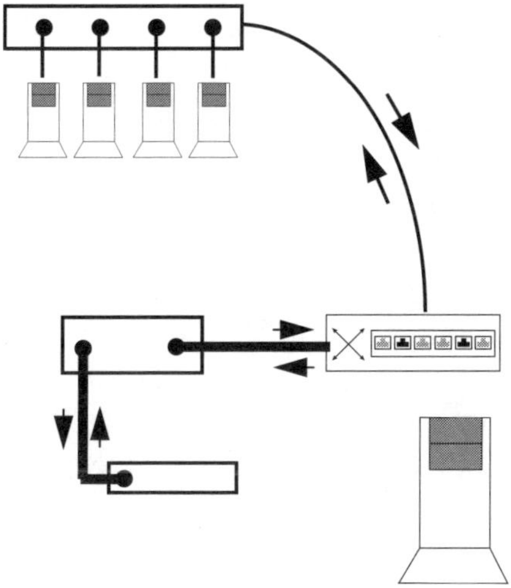

Because a switch is a bridge, you should make sure your vendor follows the Spanning Tree (transparent bridging) standard. If it uses a proprietary protocol for switch-switch communication to prevent Data Link loops, you are locked into a single-vendor network!

The Future of Switching

Many network managers are putting switches in server farms and in workgroups, using routers to connect to the backbone. We recommend this concept. Many switch vendors suggest that you do the opposite: that you switch in the core of the network and route only at the network borders. At first glance, this seems eminently foolish advice. Why would you want broadcast storms to proliferate all through your network? Isn't that why you bought routers in he first place?

If you look closely at many of these new schemes, the switches they use are devices that isolate traffic at the Network Layer (cutting-off broadcast storms). It is the opinion of the authors, as well as Scott Bradner of Harvard, if that impresses you, that any device that operates at the IP layer is functionally a router, regardless of what the vendor wants to call it.

In this book we will NOT consider the question of Layer 3 switches, IP switches, Tag Switching, Label Swapping or any other "alternatives" to routing. This book focuses on how to make your Physical and Data Link infrastructures faster - and routing, IP Switching, etc. are all Network Layer functions. *The INTEGRATING ATM class/book covers these topics. You can use these 2 books in tandem to determine both questions within the context of the same upgrade/migration decision.*

Project: Chapter 2

1. Determine which workgroups, server farms and other connections could benefit from the upgrade from hub to switch. (This assumes that you have an accurate network topology map, that you know current and near-future traffic levels, traffic and application mix on all your network segments. DO you?) You can use the information you collected in the backbone chapter to help you.

2. Determine if you want to invest in full-duplex switching at any of these locations.

3. Now, add up all the bandwidth that will be feeding into the backbone. If you don't do a worse-case scenario now, you will regret it. (Trust me.)

4. Use the number derived in #3 to determine how much bandwidth you will need on all your backbone segments. Keep this number in a secret account in the Cayman Islands because we will use it in projects later in this book. You will use it to make your ultimate upgrade decisions in the final chapter.

Referring to the information that you collected in the first chapter, concerning your backbone, you may see possible solutions to problems you uncovered, based on the products that we covered in this chapter. Put some tentative plans together. Make them tentative, because this is only Chapter 2, after all!

Summary

- Switching can help relieve congestion at server farms and in backbones and is an effective way to deliver more bandwidth to desktops as well.
- A switch is a multiport bridge and incorporates Type II repeaters. You must use bridge standards, such as Spanning Tree and Source Route Bridging, with your switches.
- Switches come in 3 types: Cut-Through, Modified Cut-Through and Store-&-Forward. You should use only the latter when attaching to the backbone.
- Full-duplex switches are available for Ethernet, Token Ring and FDDI. A full-duplex switches provides 2 full pipes from switch to switch or switch to user. Full-duplex switches require Cat. 5 UTP or fiber installations in most cases.
- Switches are available for Ethernet (at all speeds and in all forms), Token Ring and FDDI.

Review – Chapter 2

1. What device was the switch designed to replace?
2. Name the 2 common types of switches and give a good implementation example of each.
3. Does a full-duplex switch really give you twice as much bandwidth as a half-duplex switch? Why or why not?
4. What is the major advantage of full-duplex operation in Ethernet, specifically?
5. Can I have switches that run Token Ring or FDDI or is this just an Ethernet advantage?
6. Can I go from a hub to a switch with just a switch upgrade or do I have to change NICs as well?
7. What do you have to replace in your network if you are replacing hubs with full-duplex switches?
8. What do you think is the major <u>business</u> advantage of switching, from the perspective of network managers?
9. Is making the switch vs. hub decision easy or hard for you? What about replacing bridges with switches?
10. If you are currently using switches in your network, how do they interact with routers? (Do they ship addresses upstream?) Do all your infrastructure devices come from the same vendor? Are you happy about this?
11. Can you see parts of your network that would benefit from a full-duplex switch? Would you like full-duplex backbone connections? Where would you do this: campus; risers, server farms, other? (see Project)
12. (T/F) Modified cut-thru switches check the FCS.

Key Words

The words and phrases highlighted in **bold** represent key concepts in this chapter. Please take the time now to write down your own definitions of these terms, using the list below and additional paper if needed. Then compare your efforts to the training text. This is an excellent way for you to determine weak points in the breadth and depth of your understanding of this chapter.

switch
hub
repeater
Class I/II
Type I/II
collision domain
bridge
backplane
switching fabric
address isolation
cut-through
modified cut-through
store-and-forward
full-duplex
downstream
upstream
enterprise switching

3
Gigabit & Fast Ethernet

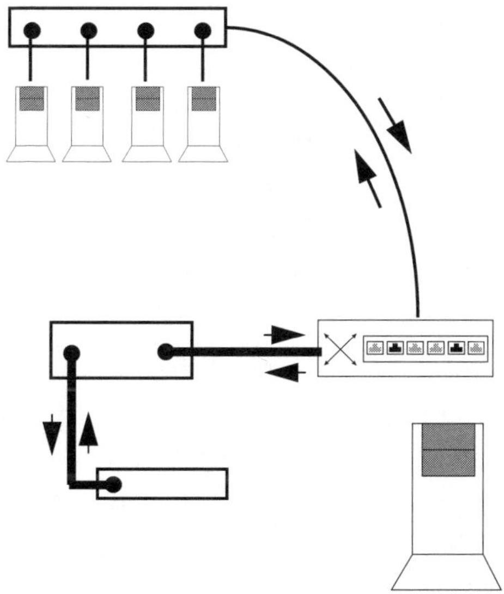

Goals of this Chapter

When you complete this chapter, you should be able to:

- ❐ Discuss the role of Ethernet switches in your network
- ❐ Define Fast Ethernet options
- ❐ Succinctly list the options for Gigabit Ethernet (GEnet)
- ❐ Discuss the conflicting needs of voice, video and data

Fast Ethernet

Fast Ethernet (802.3 100Base-T) was defined by the 802.3u working group and it has become deeply entrenched as an excellent upgrade path from 10 Mbps Ethernet. It is currently used in at least part of the network in 62% of the Fortune 1000 companies in the USA.

The original version was specified for Cat. 5 UTP, on the usual 2 pairs of UTP per RJ-45 jack. This version is referred to as **100base-TX**. The maximum segment length is 100m. and the Physical Layer line code is the same as FDDI TP-PMD (Fiber Distributed Data Interface protocols used on twisted pair Physical Medium Dependent sublayer).

The version called **100base-T4** uses 4 pairs of Cat. 3 UTP to deliver 100 Mbps over the entire spread of 8 wires. (Ordinary, standard half-duplex Ethernet - non-full-duplex - only uses one of the wires of each pair.) If you already have 4 pairs of Cat. 3 installed to your drops, this makes some sense; you have no additional wire installation cost. There is no cost savings for new cable installations compared to Cat.5; Cat.3 costs 50% less than Cat. 5 but you need twice as much wire. 100base-T4 uses **quadrature signalling**: 3 of the pairs carry 32 Mbps each and the 4th pair carries the CD arbitration. Cat. 3 can carry higher data rates without excessive crosstalk with special line codes and power components.

It was the Fast Ethernet 802.3u working group that defined the types of repeaters we discussed in Chapter 2.

Ethernet Options

Switched Ethernet

- Gives each port its own segment and collision domain
- Ports can run at different speeds & different media

Full-duplex

- Full bandwidth (10, 100, etc.) in both directions
- Requires Cat 5 UTP or fiber

Fast Ethernet 802.3 100base-xx

- Each port can be switched or shared (switch vs. hub)
- 802.3 100base-TX uses 2 pairs of Cat. 5 wire
- 802.3 100base-T4 uses 4 pairs of Cat. 3 wire
- 802.3 100base-FX uses 2 strands of multimode fiber
- UTP uses RJ-45.

More Fast Ethernet Options

The final version of Fast Ethernet gives you the longest potential backbones and the best upgrade path to Gigabit Ethernet, ATM or any other option. This is the 802.3z **100base-FX** version on 2 strands of multimode optical fiber. You can build backbones up to 2 km. long with repeaters.

You can choose to implement Fast Ethernet as a shared hub, where all the devices share a single collision domain. You can also buy a Fast Ethernet switch, where each port has 100 Mbps of its own. Most network managers consider server farms for shared or switched Fast Ethernet and implement switched Fast Ethernet in backbones - risers in particular. Fast Ethernet FX is a good choice for a campus. (Fiber is always the medium for your campus; dig once!)

If your 802.3 NICs are switchable 10/100 cards, you can upgrade to Fast Ethernet without changing cards. If your cards aren't switchable, you might want to consider switchable cards for new purchases. Some **autosensing** hubs can set each user port individually depending on the NIC you have installed, so some ports can run at 100 while others get only 10 Mbps

When you are designing a Fast Ethernet upgrade, remember that your drop ports may differ from your backbone uplink. You may have a shared hub with a switched uplink, even a full-duplex uplink.

Switch or Share?

What is a segment? This issue has become complicated by the fact that some hubs allow you to designate specific ports into a common collision domain or segment. That means that the network management console can set ports 1-5 in segment 1, ports 6-10 in segment 2 and ports 11-24 in segment 3. This is generally done in the context of a virtual LAN (**VLAN**), which creates logical LAN segmentation that transcends the physical segmentation of the wiring - and is also discussed in *LANs! LANs! LANs!*.

There are 2 Ethernet/802.3 issues that we must keep in mind as we crank up the speed of the Physical Layer: the end-to-end network diameter and the interframe gap (**IFG**). CSMA/CD makes sure that network access is fair to all participants by making sure that a station that sends a frame doesn't send another frame until it has given all the other stations on the segment (in the collision domain) a chance to see the frame that is coming by and get their own frame onto the network if they have one to send. If we did not make senders wait, a sender could send one frame after another (hog the bandwidth, in effect), the stations that were closest to the sender would have the best chance of being the next to send - you can think of other effects as well. What we have to do is set a timer, the IFG, that depends on the maximum path that the frame can take end-to-end. For 10 Mbps, IFG is 9.6 microseconds. Because Fast Ethernet runs 10 times faster, IFG must be 10 times smaller, or 0.96 microseconds. In this way, we continue to ensure that everyone has a fair chance at being the next to send a frame.

Gigabit Ethernet

The next generation of Ethernet is capable of mounting a serious competitive challenge to ATM in the LAN, delivering at least 90% of the theoretical 1Gbps. Because we are allowed to call it 802.3, we know that the MAC defines the frame in its existing form, so the software interface to IP, IPX and other popular protocols will not change.

The first standardized version of Gigabit Ethernet (802.3z) to get final approval is the fiber version, which uses **Fibre Channel** physical layer signalling on 62.5/125 multimode fiber. The link may be up to 300 meters long. The singlemode fiber version allows links of up to 3 km.

Because it is full-duplex, collision and some otherwise untenable CSMA/CD issues are eliminated. The Physical Layer is the critical layer in this case.

• Backbone switches are a good choice. On a full-duplex GEnet backbone switch, every backbone port delivers close to 1000 Mbps in each direction; you can visualize the two devices pumping a continuous flow of frames in each direction.

• No half-duplex implementation is contemplated. We could not achieve more than 500 Mbps of actual throughput without full-duplex, even if we controlled packet size and added every other finagle the 802.3 spec allows.

• GEnet NICs only make sense for servers and disk farms at this point in time.

Components of GE

Gigabit Ethernet 1000base-xx

- 1000 Mbps, full-duplex switched only
- SX Shortwave laser, multimode fiber, 300 m.
- LX Longwave laser, multimode fiber, 550 m.

or longwave laser on singlemode 3 km.

- TX Cat.5 (4 prs.)version in progress.

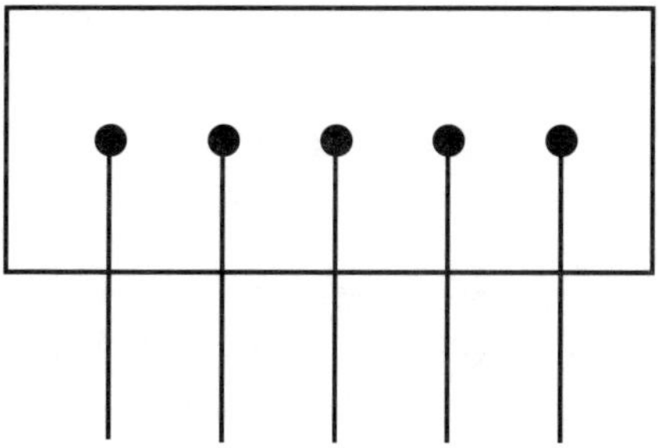

Using Gigabit Ethernet

By spring 1998, we will have a Cat.5 UTP standard, with a probable maximum segment length of 25 meters. Early vendors of Gigabit Ethernet are positioning it as a technology for backbones, server farms and disk farms that have already been provisioned with Cat.5. It will compete with ATM (with a 622 Mbps Physical Layer) for the backbone marketplace.

We should use Gigabit Ethernet for:

- Dedicated switch-to-switch connections.
- Intermediate switches with a GEnet uplink.

Gigabit Ethernet can act as the campus or riser backbone for workgroups that are using shared hubs and/or switched Fast Ethernet and original Ethernet. (Perhaps we should start calling it Classic Ethernet and charging premium prices for old NICs as antiques!)

- Variations of the bullet above, in which the local ports on the workgroup switch are shared (in VLAN segments), some are switched, some are full-duplex, etc.

Since we will eventually want to put videoconferencing and other voice/video traffic on our backbones, and achieve good performance for these systems, let us ask if Gigabit Ethernet can accomodate this traffic. Before we can start thinking about GE's suitability for voice and video traffic, we have to understand the fundamental characteristics of this traffic. That is our next topic.

GE

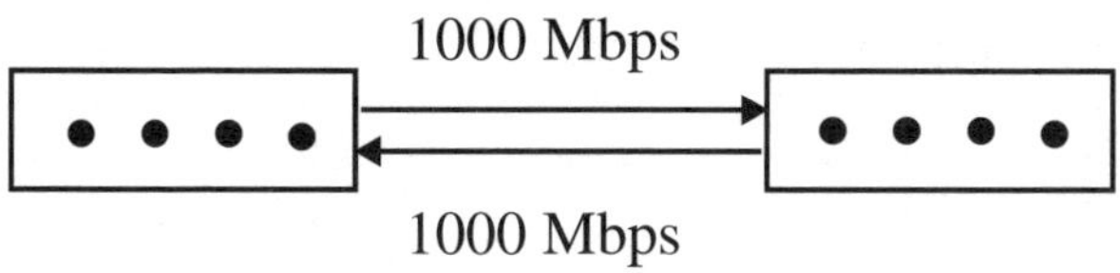

Full duplex backbone Switches

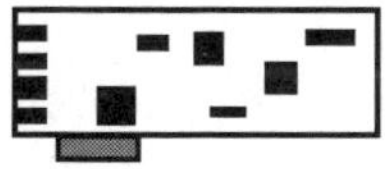

GENet NICs in end stations (Servers, Disk farms)

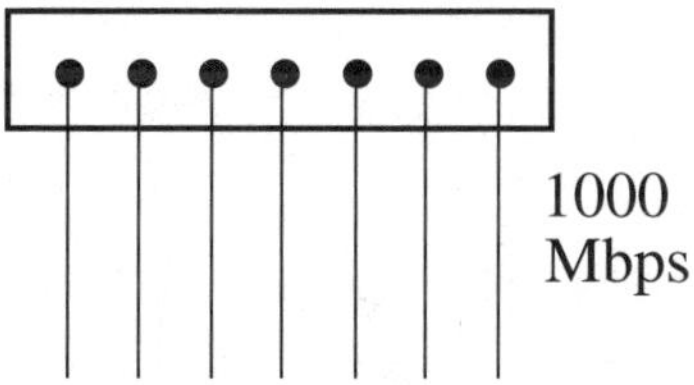

GENet Switching to the NIC

What About Voice and Video?

Essentially, realtime voice and data exist at opposite ends of a continuum of needs, as the illustration shows.

Voice is very demanding. Specifically, voice is demanding of **latency**, **jitter** and bandwidth. Latency measures end-to-end delay, which should be low. Jitter measures the variability of the delay. Jitter measures the variation in actual arrival time of a frame, compared to when the frame was expected to arrive. Jitter must be nearly zero for realtime voice. The culprit, alas, is our ears and our oh-so-clever brains, which can detect (and be annoyed by) even small variations in the arrival time of sounds when these sounds are part of words and conversations. We call realtime voice and video **isochronous** traffic, which is Greek for "same time," to indicate the importance of low jitter. A live videoconference has a voice stream and a video stream.Video is almost as demanding in its jitter requirements as voice.

Stored video clips and digitized voicemail are downloaded to your desktop as bit streams without jitter guarantees and then played in realtime after they arrive. Stored images like X-rays and CAT scans are large files and require significant amounts of bandwidth, just like non-realtime voice and video. (We will explore how ATM handles these traffic types in depth later.)

Traditional data has no jitter requirement, but requires low/no losses.

Voice and Video Needs

Live Voice

2 people call

Live Video

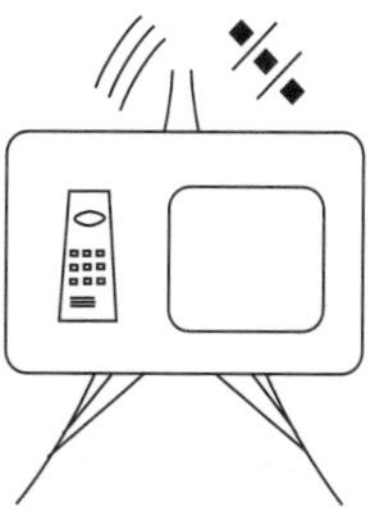

Stored Video

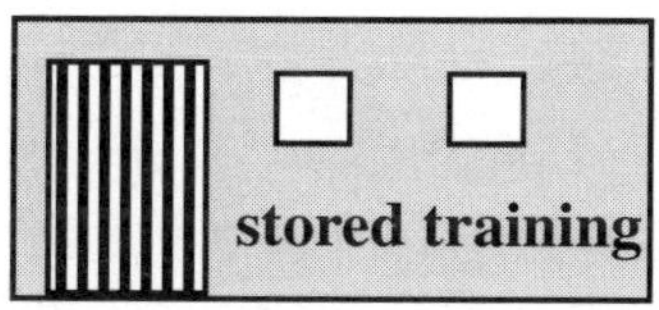

Stored Voice

Data Frames

All native traffic is digitized and stored & transported as bits

Isochronous Options

The major advantage of ATM vs. Gigabit Ethernet is that ATM was designed to carry all types of traffic, including voice and video, effectively. Are you thinking that Ethernet can carry anything that ATM can carry if you throw enough bandwidth on the pipe?

This contention is, happily for network managers everywhere, absolutely true. The only real reason for voice and video's poor performance on less-than-gigabit Ethernet is the fact of congestion. Since Ethernet has no really efficient way to give voice traffic the near-zero jitter guarantees that it needs, a congested network will not give you good voice performance. If there is plenty of bandwidth, you will get very good videoconferencing performance over Ethernet. A full analysis of the pros and cons awaits you in Chapter 6. In addition, the *Integrating ATM With Legacy LANs* book discusses IP's new v.6 and its support for isochronous traffic, as well as MPOA, IP switching and related subjects. Because this is a barely-birthed technology, vendors are including all sorts of non-standard "enhancements" to accomodate (differentiate) isochronous traffic as it travels through their switches.

Project: Chapter 3

Return to the work that you did in Chapter 1 in examining your backbone.

1. Beginning with your campus or inter-building backbone, can you see any use for Gigabit Ethernet? Remember that you can get 2 kilometer runs on fiber.

2 Look at your building risers. Have you identified any needs for GEnet here? Look at your projected bandwidth needs. Very few technologies are running at these projected speeds.

3. Now look at the segments that you have identified as requiring a bandwidth boost. Are any of them suitable for GEnet?

4. Are there any opportunities for Fast Ethernet to be of use to you in boosting bandwidth? It is relatively stable, having been available for several years, and is available from many vendors. Most Ethernet cards are 10/100 switchable, so you will only need to consider switch/hub replacements.

Summary

- ❐ The 802.3 subcommittee has approved various versions of Fast Ethernet. 100base-TX runs on 2 pairs of Cat. 5 UTP. 100base-T4 runs on 4 pairs of Cat. 3-5 UTP. 100base-FX uses 2 strands of multimode fiber. All versions use the FDDI line codes.
- ❐ The 802.3 subcommittee has approved Gigabit Ethernet (GEnet) on multimode optical fiber. It must run full-duplex. Collisions are impossible so the CD circuitry is essentially disabled.
- ❐ Fast Ethernet is very popular as a backbone, for campuses and risers, and also as a high-speed pipe into storage and server farms.
- ❐ Gigabit Ethernet is expected to provide an upgrade for networks that need more than 100 Mbps in the backbone and the storage/server farms.
- ❐ Any fast network can provide adequate support for isochronous traffic - provided that maximum traffic levels NEVER allow congestion to occur. In addition, both GEnet and IP designers are working on isochronous support issues.

Review – Chapter 3

1. Can 100base-T4 Fast Ethernet be converted to full-duplex operation? Why or why not?
2 What is the 802.3 10baseT Physical Layer line code? Why do you think the 802.3u subcommittee chose TP-PMD's line code for Fast Ethernet?
3. If you currently have Cat.3 installed to the desktop, do you have any options in this chapter? Would it be cost-effective to put in another medium? Which one and why?
4. Why does the IFG change when the bps increases?
5. Some people say that GEnet "isn't really Ethernet" or "doesn't really conform to the original Ethernet concept." What do they mean? (Be specific.) Do you agree?
6. List the media choices for Fast Ethernet and GEnet.
7. How would you guarantee jitter and latency as voice/video require it if you try to carry room-system videoconferencing on any version of Ethernet?
8. If you decide to use GEnet for your campus backbone, what hardware elements do you need to purchase? What about your risers? What about your server/storage farms? Make complete lists, with up/downlinks.
9. Could GEnet ever make sense to the desktop? Where?
10. Why do current scenarios embrace only full-duplex switching for GEnet? (Be technically specific.)
11. (T/F) GEnet uses token-passing because it uses FDDI's Physical Layer spec, including the same line code.
12. (T/F) GEnet is used by 62% of non-SNA networks.

Key Words

The words and phrases highlighted in **bold** represent key concepts in this chapter. Please take the time now to write down your own definitions of these terms, using the list below and additional paper if needed. Then compare your efforts to the training text. This is an excellent way for you to determine weak points in the breadth and depth of your understanding of this chapter.

Fast Ethernet

Gigabit Ethernet

100base-TX

100base-T4

100base-FX

1000base-FX

Quadrature Signalling

latency

jitter

Fibre Channel

isochronous

IFG

autosensing

VLAN

4
ATM Technology

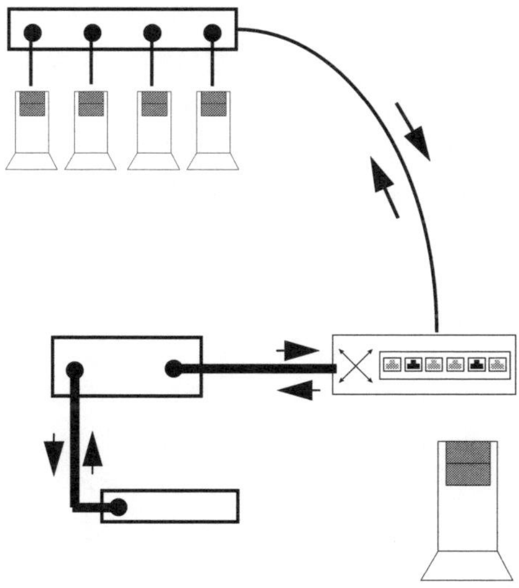

Goals of this Chapter

When you complete this chapter, you should be able to:

- ❒ List the 5 classes of ATM service and describe what kind of traffic each one is designed for
- ❒ Discuss the specific traffic descriptors of the 3 classes of service for isochronous traffic
- ❒ Explain QOS and how it differs from traffic description
- ❒ Explain Traffic Conformance and leaky buckets

Why ATM?

There are 2 answers to this: high-speed network segments and isochronous traffic support.

ATM accounted for 10% of all new backbones being installed in the Fortune 1000 in the USA in 1996. Most network managers around the world who are surveyed for their backbone migration preferences said that ATM was their top choice - before the development of Gigabit Ethernet. Now the situation is more murky. In addition, since ATM was originally designed to serve the needs of voice, video and data integration, ATM constitutes the top technology choice for network managers who want to integrate live videoconferencing, either room-style or desktop-style, into the overall network.

ATM is fundamentally different from any other network you have ever encountered, as well as more complex and more powerful. We need this complexity to deliver the support that isochronous traffic needs.

In this chapter, we will begin our exploration of ATM by looking at the traffic issues that multimedia introduces and continue with the traffic types that you will put on your ATM network as you begin to videoconference.

Just like any other LAN access technology, ATM turns a raw bit stream into some kind of standard LAN frame, which in ATM's case are called **cells**. Devices that take in cells and switch them are called ATM switches. Devices that take in traditional LAN frames or raw audio/video streams and turn them into cells are called **edge or border devices**.

What is ATM?

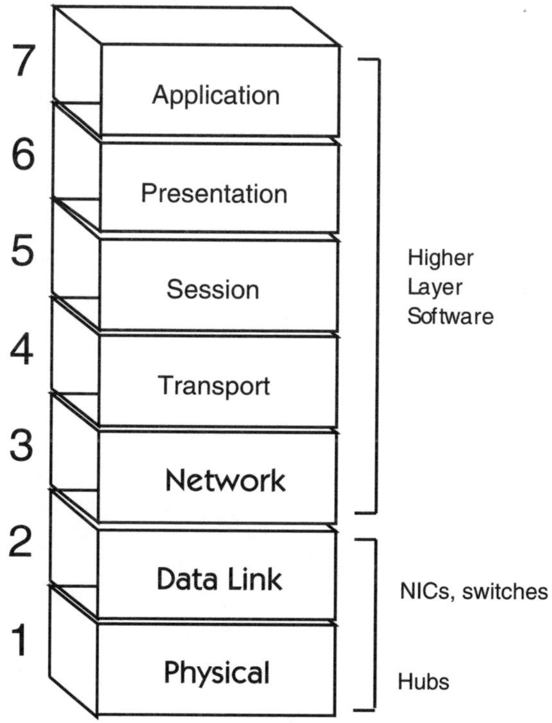

ATM is an option for the Physical and Data Link Layers of your network - which includes adaptor cards, hubs and switches. It is the Physical Layer choice you make that determines how fast ATM goes; we explore these choices in the next chapter.

Why 53 Octets?

ATM cells are only 53 octets long, of which 48 (data) or less (voice/video) are actual payload. Why so small?

Voice traffic streams can't wait, slowly filling up a cell with digitized bits, without impacting jitter expectations. For voice, frames should be as small as possible. Data's needs are exactly the obverse; data frames need to be as large as possible so that the ratio of overhead to actual user data can be as small as possible.

When designing ATM, the ITU had to compromise between voice and data proposals. They also had to keep in mind that ATM cells have to fit into a SONET or SDH Physical Layer frame an integer number of times. (SONET/SDH is the super high-speed synchronous Physical Layer ATM assumes is under it.) The only number that fit all these criteria was 53. The ITU chose a fixed-size cell to make switching faster, executable in hardware and easy to speed up by the additional of new switching elements. (A lot of processing is wasted in today's technology because of variable length Ethernet/etc. frames.)

What ATM does is take native digital streams of voice, video and data and put them into tiny, fixed-size cells, with a header that indicates what kind of service the cell has been guaranteed by the network. Let's look at these types of service that the network must guarantee to its incoming voice, video and data streams.

What is Different About ATM?

The network must guarantee the very different needs of all the traffic types.

Live video and voice need low latency and constant jitter.

Data needs low losses - because one lost cell can mean an entire large Ethernet frame needs to be re-sent!

Needs of Traffic

Low Latency
No jitter

Low Latency
No jitter

Data

No losses (loss of 1 cell requires retransmission of hundreds of additional cells).

Traffic Contracts

Every other LAN you have ever worked with has followed the same basic rule: the traffic-generating devices in the network (users, servers, mainframes) send traffic whenever they feel like it and the LAN has to deal with what it gets. It might be congested and end up throwing out some frames, but it only gets to respond ex post facto to what the attached devices throw at it.

In ATM, the situation is entirely different!

ATM insists on **traffic contracts**. The ATM network is asked to sign a traffic contract with a traffic source whenever a new connection through the network is set up. This contract is far more serious than the "we'll do our best" connectionless network effort.You tell the network exactly what you need in terms of service and the network examines its resources and says "yes, I'll take this contract" or "no, I won't take this contract." In technical terms: the network will reject a proposed connection if its existing network resources are not sufficient to allow it to guarantee specific service levels. Existing network resources are what's left after considering all the other contracts that the network has already signed with other devices before you arrived with your request.

The traffic contract for data flows, in most networks today, is negotiated on behalf of the actual sender by a border device, that translates between the ATM backbone and the Ethernet ed users, servers and other devices. These edge/border devices can be incorporated in boxes that also route, switch, bridge, gateway and perform other network functions.

Traffic Contracts

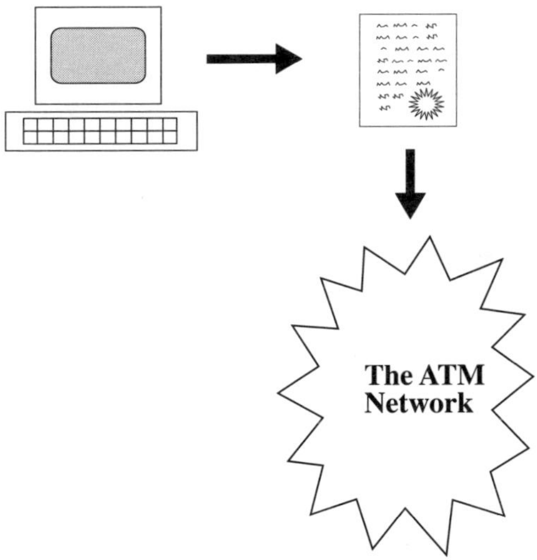

Service Guarantees

The traffic contracts the network negotiates come in one of 5 types. Constant Bit Rate (**CBR**), for live voice, has the most stringent contract. Variable Bit Rate (**VBR**) comes in two types for live or stored video. And there is Available Bit Rate (**ABR**) and Unassigned Bit Rate (**UBR**) for data. Each contract chooses one of these classes. Each class' definition begins with traffic descriptors. The **traffic descriptors** we use to characterize the traffic are:

- **Peak Cell Rate** (**PCR**)
- **Sustainable Cell Rate** (**SCR**)
- **Minimum Cell Rate** (**MCR**)
- **Maximum Burst Size** (**MBS**)

CBR Voice, as the most demanding traffic type, requires iron-clad guarantees of service in all these categories. Video requires only some of them. Data will generally take whatever it can get, be grateful and never complain.

The foursome listed above are the **Source Traffic Descriptors** (**STD**s) - the description of the traffic created by the source device. The **Transit Traffic Descriptors (TDDs)** are the STDs, plus the Cell Delay Variation Tolerance (**CDVT**) — jitter tolerance, basically — and QOS values. TTDs describe the traffic as it transits through the network.

In the next pages, we will look at how the traffic types differ with respect to these descriptors.

Traffic Descriptors

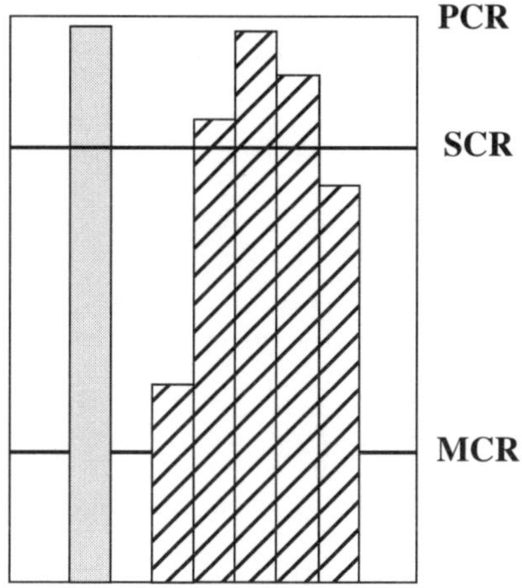

Peak Cell Rate is the maximum cell rate allowed.

Sustainable Cell Rate is the AVERAGE cell rate. If the traffic source is pumping out cells at the peak rate all the time, the sustainable and peak rates will be the same.

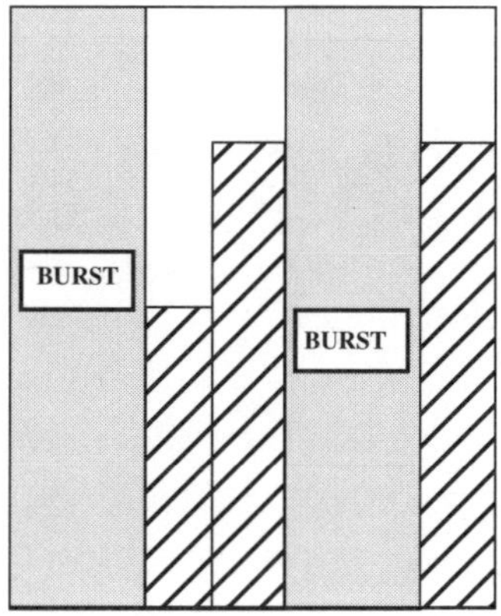

Maximum Burst Size is the maximum length that you want the network to accept cells at the peak rate. Running at your peak rate is **bursting**.

Minimum Cell Rate is the minimum cell rate that the network guarantees to carry.

CBR

Constant Bit Rate traffic requires:

- bandwidth allocation end-to-end

What this really means is that bandwidth requirements are fixed at PCR for the duration of the connection.The source can send data up to PCR for any length. If the source is not sending at PCR every moment, some bandwidth has been allocated and is not being used, just as in a leased line WAN. MCR equals PCR, and you are assumed to be bursting 100% of the time. The network absolutely allocates these resources to your CBR connection, regardless of whether you are actually sending cells or not.

We say that a CBR connection emulates realtime telephony; this is exactly the application for CBR in WANs. We don't put our telephone calls across LANs these days, so you may wonder why we would use CBR in a LAN. After all, CBR is like a leased line across your LAN. The answer is that the audio portion of a videoconference is realtime telephony, whether it is room-to-room or desktop-to-desktop.

CBR

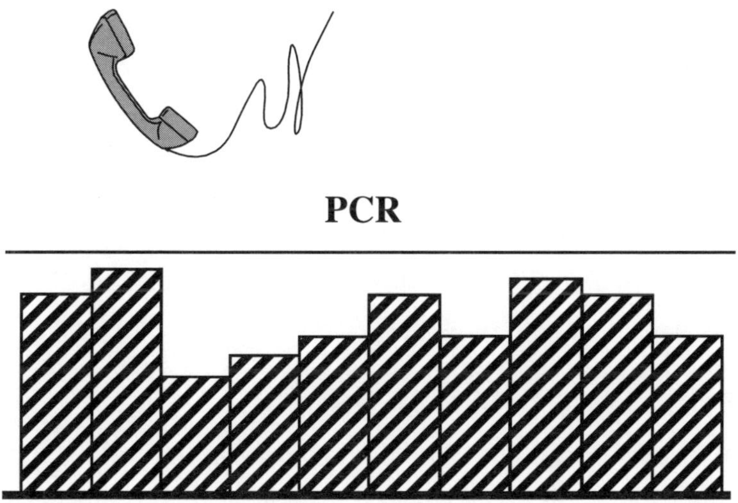

VBR

VBR-rt (realtime) requires a small and controlled delay. It specifies PCR, MBS and SCR, but it assumes that the traffic flow will not be constant. (If it were, you'd use CBR.) You can burst up to PCR for the maximum burst rate, but must average no more than SCR for the duration of the connection.

The variation in the incoming bit rate means (from the network's perspective) that the same physical connection can carry multiple multiplexed VBR-rt connections. The video portion of live videoconferencing, either from a desktop or a larger room-system, uses VBR-rt connections. If you are doing a "broadcast" in realtime from a central video server to multiple sites for training purposes, the video portion is VBR-rt also. A videoconference requires 2 connections: 1 CBR and 1 VBR-rt.

VBR-nrt (non-realtime)

In these applications, you don't have network delay requirements that are as strict as in **rt**. Bandwidth requirements vary over the course of the connection. Traffic descriptors are PCR, MBS and SCR. You can multiplex various connections over the same physical connection, just as in **rt**.

You use VBR-nrt connections for transmission of static images (medical x-rays, for example), stored video or video-on-demand in which you download entire files to a desktop and then play them locally in realtime. The latter application is popular for training because your employees or students can access video-based materials from a server on their own preferred schedule.

VBR Multiplexing

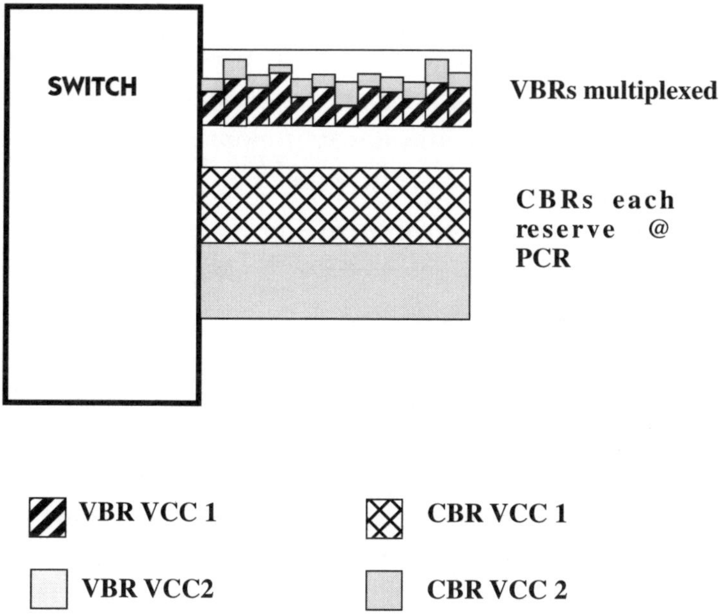

Service for Data - UBR & ABR

The first class of service developed for data was UBR. The problem with UBR - and it's a whopper! - is the lack of an effective mechanism for fairness of access. If the network gets congested, you want everyone to slow down equally. Then everyone gets a little slower response, but no one hogs the bandwidth just because they got on the network first and no one is shut out because someone else is being selfish. Since UBR doesn't have a fairness mechanism, most vendors don't implement it.

The better option is ABR, because of the existence of a congestion-response mechanism through Resource Management (**RM**) cells. After six data cells on a particular logical connection, the switch creates an RM cell as the 7th cell. The RM cell travels to the destination and back, testing for congestion in the path. If a switch is congested, it will mark a bit in the RM cell. The sender gets the RM return cells and sees that congestion is occurring somewhere and cranks back. Presumably, so will every other device, based on the testimony of their own RM cells. When RM cells begin to round-trip with no congestion notification, the senders begin to increase their traffic until RMs signal congestion again.

ABR specifies only PCR and MCR, and is delay tolerant. However, the QOS specifies data's intolerance for loss.

The latest version of RM says that the network manager can create **virtual sources** and **virtual destinations** for these logical flows. If each switch is an endpoint for congestion feedback, the feedback loop is much smaller and faster.

RM Cells

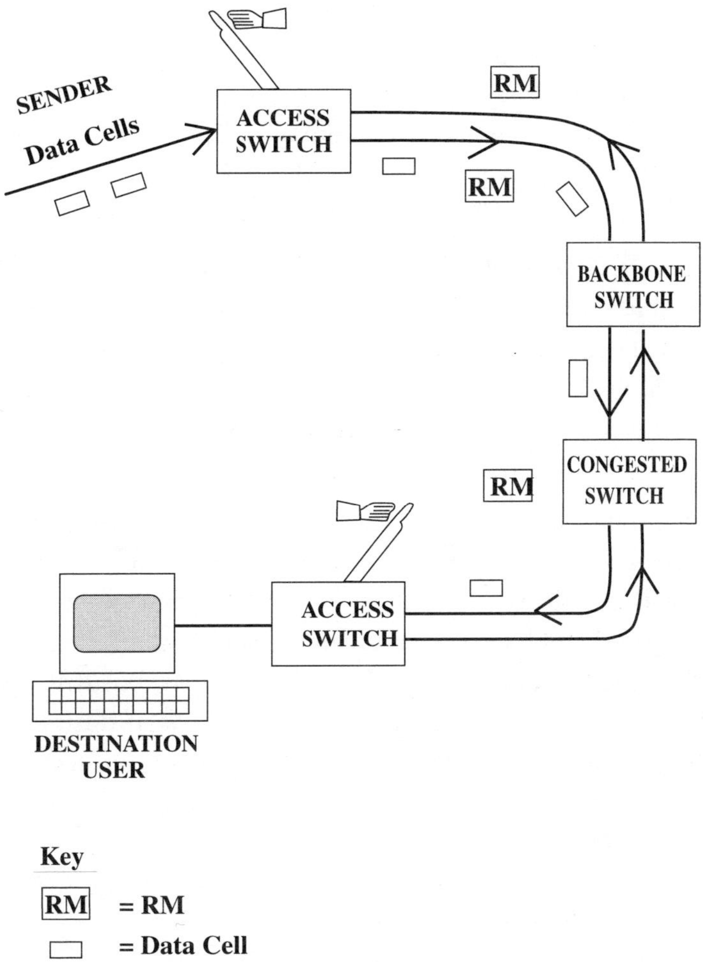
SENDER
Data Cells
ACCESS SWITCH
RM
RM
BACKBONE SWITCH
CONGESTED SWITCH
RM
ACCESS SWITCH
DESTINATION USER
Key
RM = RM
= Data Cell

Quality of Service and CDVT

Quality of Service (**QOS**) measures errored cells, mean cell delay, maximum cell transfer delay, maximum end-to-end transfer delay, and cell loss ratio. In other words, how much "failure to perform" is the network allowed to get away with before the sender gets really mad and demands restitution? You probably have had a vague idea that QOS meant something like latency or pre-allocated bandwidth. These important ideas are actually determined by the STDs and CDVT.

The traffic contract is the TTDs and a way of dealing with cells that violate their traffic contract. So far, we have defined STDs and QOS. Let's talk about jitter, or to be more precise, CDVT, which specifies the receiving client's tolerance for variation in arrival times of cells. CBR and VBR-rt require consistent intervals between cells.

To test network conformance to the transit contract: We expect a cell to arrive on the CBR or VBR-rt connection every **w** milliseconds. CDVT determines the window of "a little bit early, a little bit late" on either side of **w** that is still considered OK. A switch that gets a cell a little too early, but still within CDVT, can hold the cell until it is exactly **w**, if desired. If it falls outside of the CDVT gray-zone, it is nonconforming.

CDVT

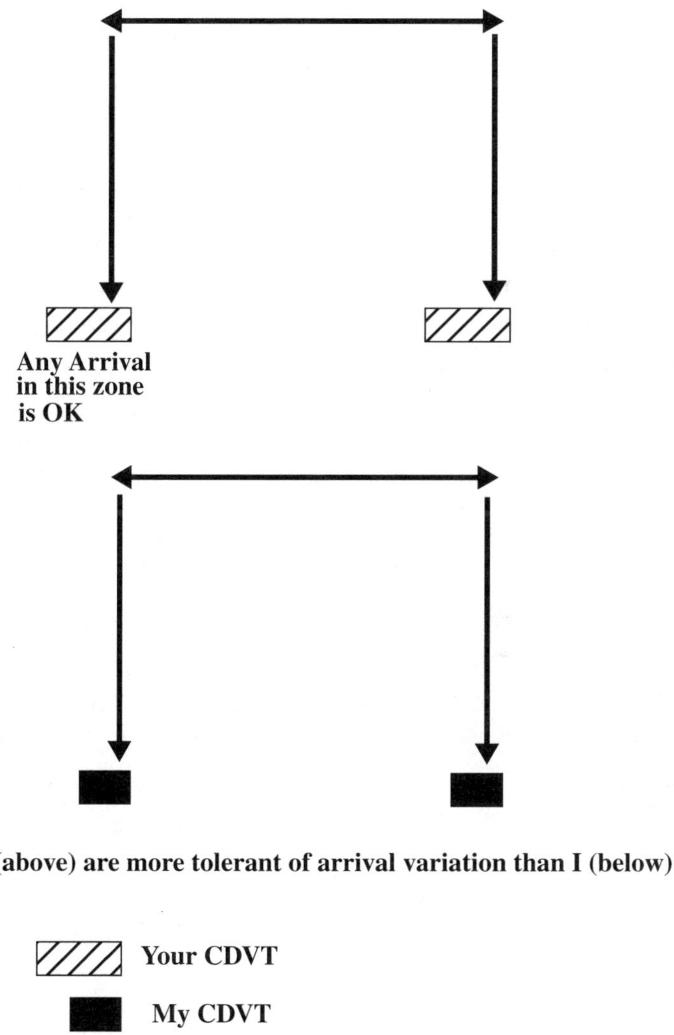
Any Arrival
in this zone
is OK
You (above) are more tolerant of arrival variation than I (below)
Your CDVT
My CDVT

Is This Cell Conforming?

CDVT is used to determine the network's conformance to the transit portion of the contract. The other partner in this contract is the sender. The ATM network promises to deliver service as long as the end user sender abides by its side of the contract and stays within the **access conformance** definition, the last element of the traffic contract.

In practice, access conformance is mostly an issue for data, not isochronous traffic, because we do not know in advance how much traffic ABR will try to send with a particular logical connection number. If the ABR sender sends more cells than the contract called for on that specific logical connection, the access switch will, depending on the vendor, flip the Cell Loss Priority (**CLP**) bit in the cell header to "1" or it will discard the cell. A cell that is marked non-conforming (1) in the CLP field can be discarded by the network later on if congestion occurs; it is a signal to the network that this cell violated the access part of the contract and the network has no obligations with respect to it.

The proposal the ATM Forum approved for access control is known technically as the Generic Cell Rate Algorithm (**GCRA**) and more popularly as the **leaky bucket**. The bucket has a hole in the bottom. The larger the hole, the larger the number of drips that will fall through every **w**. Change drip to cell and you have ABR's access control. We expect a cell to fall through the hole in the bucket at intervals of **w**. If it drips too many cells, or the drip is delayed too long, we have either a non-conforming or a tossed-out cell.

Leaky Bucket

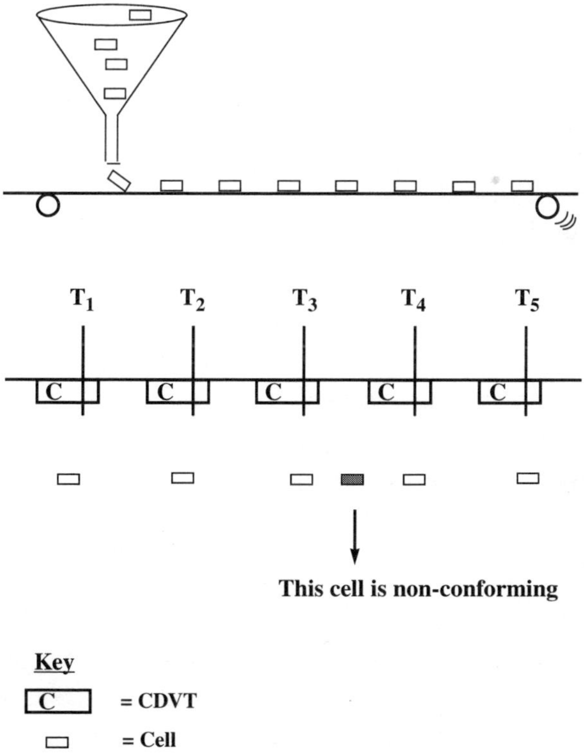

The leaky bucket tests cell flows by using PCR + CVDT or SCR + MBS, depending on what's more appropriate.

ABR Rate-Based Congestion Management

In addition to thinking about transit conformance of cells that are in transit, and access conformance for cells that are entering the network, ABR VCs also present us with the challenge of congestion management. In an ABR situation, congestion occurs at a switch because too many ABR VCs are throwing cells at the switch (sending at PCR). RM cells are an example of a **rate-based congestion management** system. Rate-based systems are well-suited to WANs, where congestion builds more slowly than in LANs.

The ATM Forum chose this, rejecting a competing, technically-better for LANs (but late) proposal for a **credit-based congestion management** system. In a credit-based system, no switch sends unless it is SURE that the downstream receiver has capacity available, so we prevent congestion from occurring. Each sending switch or edge device has a send and receive buffer for each individual VC.

We start with the receiver edge device giving the switch closest to it a "credit" balance, representing the # of cells that it can accept into its now-empty receive buffer. In effect you are passing a credit balance to your next upstream neighbor. Each switch passes this credit balance upstream until it comes to the sending edge device. When the sender gets the credit balance, it sends. Now, as each switch receives cells, it must send them on to the next switch downstream. It can then send more credits upstream to represent the amount of additional cells it can now accept into its emptying receive buffer.

Quantum Flow Control

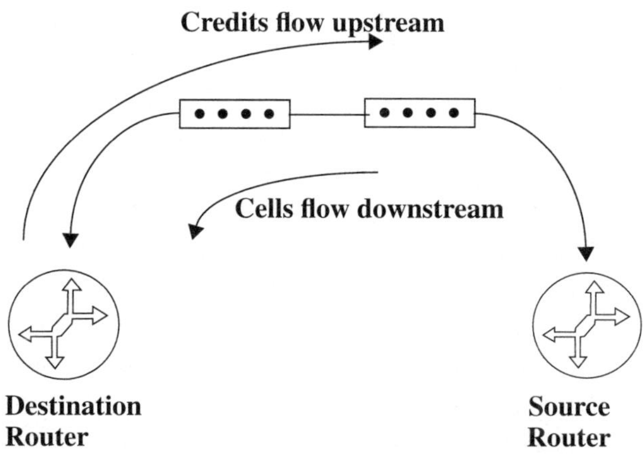

"Upstream" here means toward the source of the traffic, wherever it is, NOT toward the backbone.

"Downstream" similarly means toward the destination.

The credit-based folks have resubmitted their original proposal to the ATM Forum under the new name of Quantum Flow Control (**QFC**).

Project: Congestion Management

In this exercise, we will think about the 2 basic strategies for dealing with congestion on ABR links - rate-based (after the fact) and credit-based (prevention).

1: Make a diagram of 3 LAN switches, 2 edge devices (which may also be routers) and 5 ABR VCs with appropriate cell flows. The ABR traffic is multiplexed on a single physical channel. Use the opposite page if you like. Use different colors or any other way of differentiating the 5 flows.

2. Think about ABR traffic. Does a particular desktop/server communication send cells at the same rate all the time? Come up with a SPECIFIC traffic scenario that could create momentary congestion at the middle switch. For example, the server starts a file download on ABR #2, while another user is downloading a bunch of email on ABR #3, etc.

3. Be specific so you can really visualize how this could happen. You want to make it really clear to yourself that whereas CBR preallocates bandwidth for its worst-case scenario, ABR is playing a statistical game - without much to go on. Remember, ABR specifies only peak cell rate and minimum cell rate. You have NO idea when bursts may occur and how long they will last. (VBR also plays a statistical game, but with much more information, so congestion should not occur.)

4. Create a feedback loop from the edge device on the left to the first enterprise/network switch. Do the same for the right edge device and the switch connected to it. Create another feedback loop from the first network switch to the third. You now have 3 feedback loops and 3 virtual source/destination pairs for each ABR circuit, for a total of 15. How does this allow the network to respond to congestion faster? Keep in mind that it's the entry devices that are the ultimate sources of trouble (bursts of cells), so having a very rapid feedback loop to them is especially important. We need to tell them "stop!" as soon as congestion looms. In this scenario, can we?

5. Put more feedback loops in this network. Where are they? Why did you make the choices you did?

6. Now draw another diagram and experiment with the QFC concepts. Draw the send and receive buffers in each switch and follow each group of 100 cells as they flow through each switch. What happens to each buffer? Did you remember that buffers are unique to each VC? (You do not have a single buffer for a physical link. What would happen if you did? Hint: Think about the fair access issue.)

LAN congestion can blow up more quickly than a flash-flood down an arroyo, because of the unpredictable and bursty nature of traffic, so it is better to prevent it than to try to cope with it after the fact. With all its advantages of actually preventing congestion (so important to LANs), you might wonder why QFC has not been adopted by many LAN vendors. Can you think of a reason why a LAN vendor would prefer rate-based congestion control?

Congestion is a key issue for ABR flows in LANs, as we'll explore in Chapter 5.

Make Some Pictures

Summary

- ATM networks negotiate a traffic contract with the device that needs service. The 5 types of contract are different for voice, video and data.
- The types of contracts differ in the importance they give to end-to-end error control, to jitter and to how bursty the traffic is expected to be. Many specific parameters determine every aspect of the contract.
- No traffic can be sent from sender to receiver until a specific path has been created from sender to receiver, with all intervening switches prepared for the traffic flow.
- The addresses on an ATM cell are locally, not globally, significant. We call them labels and we swap them just as we do in frame relay.
- We decide whether or not a cell conforms to its contract; if it does not, the network can throw it out or tag it as nonconforming.
- The 2 competing congestion control schemes are rate-based and credit based. The ATM Forum chose a rate-based scheme called RM, but may also embrace QFC at a later date.

Review – Chapter 4

1. What are the 5 most common classes of ATM service? List their three-letter acronyms.

2-6. For each of the classes above, list the Traffic Descriptors that are used with each one.

7. Why is UBR being abandoned in favor of ABR? Be as specific as possible.

8. Describe the end-to-end flow of a Resource Management cell.

9. What 2 layers of the ATM network must interface with Ethernet? What layers interface with Token Ring?

10. If I am videoconferencing, how many traffic streams am I producing? Is this concentrated into one ATM class of service or more? What class(es) are used?

11. How does CBR differ from VBR-rt?

12. Define QOS, being as specific as possible.

13. What does CDVT measure?

14. What class of service has the most stringent requirements for CDVT? WHY?

15. Why is QOS and CDVT included in the traffic contract?

16. What determines if a cell is conforming?

17. Does conformance make sense as part of the traffic contract? Why or why not?

18. Some analysts say that ATM caters to voice and video, but short-changes the needs of data. Do you agree? Why or why not?

Key Words

The words and phrases highlighted in **bold** represent key concepts in this chapter. Please take the time now to write down your own definitions of these terms, using the list below and additional paper if needed. Then compare your efforts to the training text. This is an excellent way for you to determine weak points in the breadth and depth of your understanding of this chapter.

cell
traffic contract
PCR
SCR
MCR
MBS
burst
RM
leaky bucket
CBR
VBR-rt
VBR-nrt
ABR
QFC
border device
isochronous
CDVT
UBR
STD
TTD
QOS
traffic descriptor
access conformance
edge device
virtual source
virtual destination
rate-based congestion control
credit-based congestion control
GCRA

5
ATM Advanced Topics

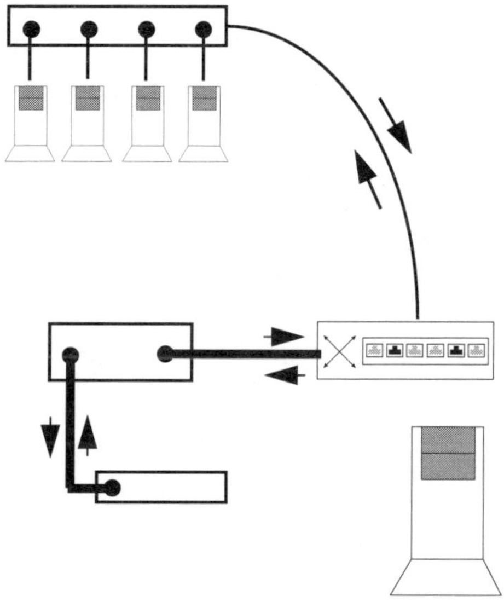

Goals of this Chapter

When you complete this chapter, you should be able to:

- ❒ Discuss how a VPC and VCC are assigned to a traffic flow
- ❒ Explain how VCCs can drop in and out of a VP
- ❒ Explain 5 of the traffic management options for ATM
- ❒ List the Physical Layer options for ATM LANs
- ❒ Discuss the importance of the Anchorage Accords for ATM LAN development

Virtual Paths & Channels

In the last chapter, we explored traffic types, contract elements and ATM basics. In this chapter, we will look at how ATM cells get switched through an entirely ATM network, what cells look like, congestion and access management and other traffic and error control matters. To begin with, we need to define how ATM cells get from place to place. We call the virtual circuit that we build through the network of switches a Virtual Channel Connection (**VCC**).

As a way of helping ATM switches to switch cells more quickly, especially in WANs, we have another logical entity called a Virtual Path Connection (**VPC**), a group of VCCs, all of which must be of the same traffic type (ABR, CBR, etc.). If a user requests a new VBR-rt connection for the video portion of a videoconference, the configuration server that allocates new VCCs can look in the VPCs dedicated to VBR-rt for an available circuit number. (Exact details of the configuration and setup process are covered in *Integrating ATM With Legacy LANs*.) The configuration server (software) can be resident anywhere in the network, depending on the vendor.

Having a larger entity above the individual VCCs allows faster switching within switches. In a WAN, it is helpful, for example, to put all the voice heading to Chicago on one VP, then instruct the switches to switch all the VCCs inside the incoming VPC to the new outgoing VPC dedicated to the next stage of the trip to Chicago. Within a switch, if all the VCCs are not destined for the same outbound VPC, the individual VCCs switch in and out of the VPC as the individual flow was originally set up.

Virtual Channels

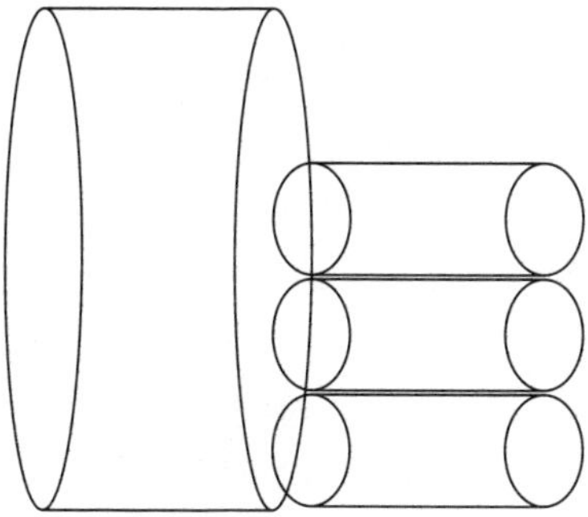

VPC3 for CBR

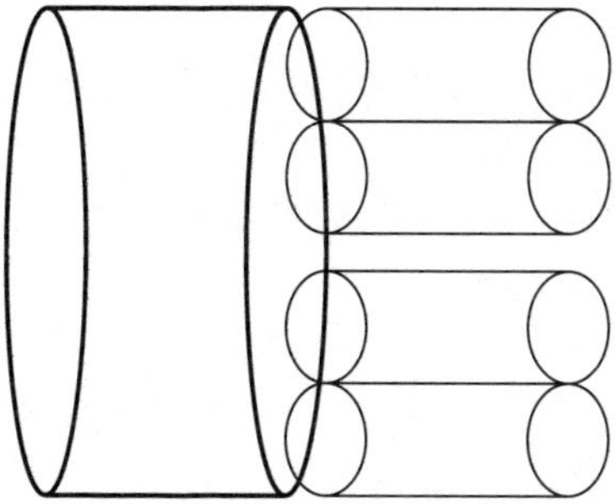

VPC4 for ABR (all Ethernet)

Setting Up a Traffic Flow

What we do in ATM networks is we create end-to-end virtual circuits to carry the traffic, and we provision each ATM switch to swap from one locally-significant label to another along the way. For instance, we start with a local switch that gets a circuit setup request for CBR service. This switch looks at its list of available CBR virtual (not physical, please note) circuits and sees that outgoing VCC #5 on the CBR VPC #2 is available. It transmits the setup request to the next switch along the path toward the destination. Along the way, each switch notes the VCC that is incoming, checks to see if it has a CBR outgoing VCC available and tentatively assigns the new request to it.

If all the switches along the way have CBR bandwidth available, the request will return through each switch, confirming what had been tentative VCC assignments.

Now look at what will happen to the user traffic when the CBR VCC becomes active for the phone call or audio portion of a live videoconference. As each cell is released to the first switch, it comes in with a particular VCC # attached. At the switch, the incoming VCC number is swapped for the appropriate outgoing number (the circuit number that was allocated to this sender at circuit setup time). Each switch will look at the incoming number, consult its table of "equivalencies" and put the new outgoing VPC/VCC numbers in the cell header.

Label Swapping

The circuit/path numbers are not **globally-significant**; we say that ATM VCCs and VPCs are **locally-significant**, because they are just convenient labels to indicate what incoming and outgoing stream the cell belongs to. They are NOT constant numbers representing the actual sender and receiver. The actual sender and receiver ATM addresses are not attached to the cells while traffic is flowing; they are involved only in circuit setup.

The process of taking the incoming VPC/VCC off and putting the outgoing VPC/VCC on is called **label-swapping.**

All the elements of this network can move at high speed because the transfer of cells is a simple process of reading a short address, looking at a table to see which output port and new address the cell needs, then changing the address and sending the cell to the appropriate output port. We swap the incoming label (address) for the outgoing label, without doing any thinking or deciding.

Label swapping is a technical term used in ATM, Frame Relay and other technologies that use virtual circuit numbers, not globally-unique "real" addresses. In Frame Relay or other VC-based WANs, what happens at each incoming switch is we take the incoming DLCI, look at the table and see that DLCI 4 on port 3 should be swapped to DLCI 6 on port 4. ATM label-swapping works the same way, with VCCs and VPCs instead of DLCIs.

Types of VCCs and VPCs

In order to accomodate the needs of network management and control – setting up and taking down the VCCs and VPCs, for example – we define some VCC and VPC numbers as dedicated to just these functions. If the VPC is dedicated to network control, then every VCC inside it is dedicated to network control, because all VCCs must be of the same type - control being a type. The network manager will determine how many VPCs to dedicate to each traffic type. You might end up underprovisioning some of the traffic types, and will have to adjust as you get more experience with your ATM network.

Data VCCs, which carry user payloads of voice, video and packet data, are generally defined as bidirectional. Among **Control VCC**s, some are unidirectional and some are bidirectional. Devices that communicate via a 2-directional VCC can be either sender or receiver. If devices are communicating via a 1-directional VCC, it means that the control device either sends or receives, but can't do both on the same VCC.

Remember: these are logical connections, not physical connections. If we talk about "directions," we just mean that the client can either send or receive with the specified VCC number on the cells. If a device is set to only send on a particular VCC, it will not understand that VCC number on an incoming cell, and will throw it out.

Label Swapping

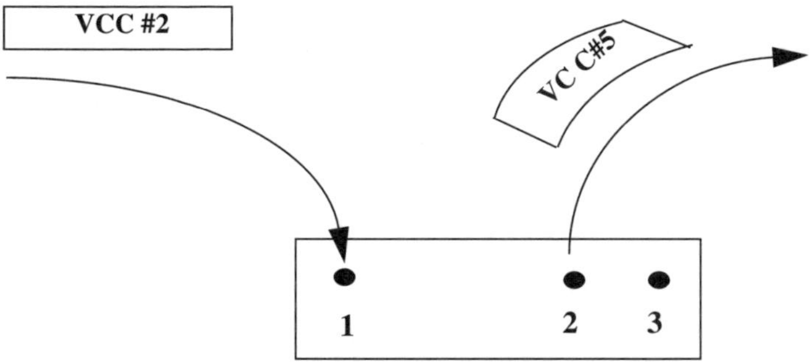

Types of VCs

Unidirectional

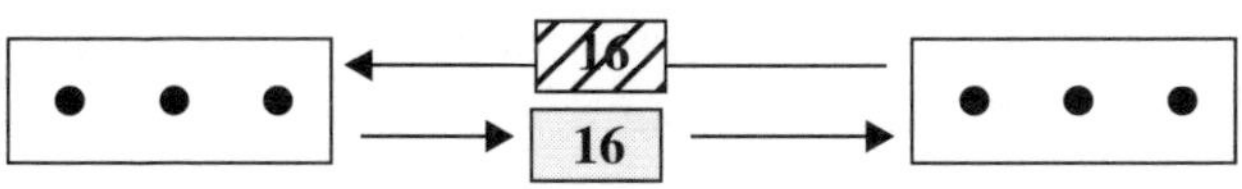

16 out ≠ 16 in

Bidirectional

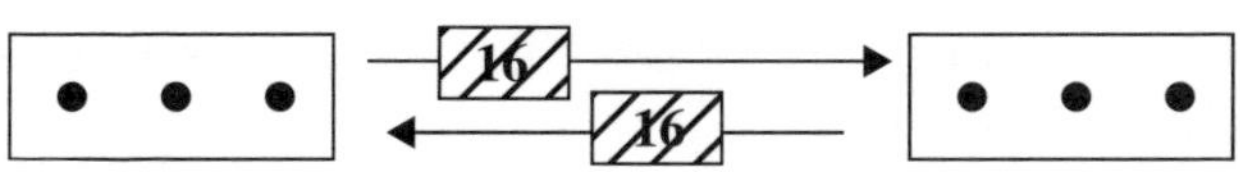

16 out =16 in

Bidirectional VCCs are almost always for control/signalling. Data VCCs are almost always unidirectional, so an incoming cell with VCC 16 is not the same flow as an outgoing cell labelled VCC 16

The ATM Model

The ATM Model, developed by the ITU as part of the larger Broadband ISDN model, includes:

• The Physical Layer functions to support transmission across the medium, whatever it is.

• The ATM Layer defines how cells are transported across the network, using VCCs, etc.

• The **Adaptation Layer** defines how raw traffic flows are transformed (adapted) into cells. In particular, the Segmentation and Reassembly (**SAR**) sublayer functions as a translator from Ethernet frames into ABR cells, of telephony into CBR cells and video streams into VBR cells.

The ITU originally defined the AALs as Classes (A-E); you will also see Classes 1-5 referred to, especially by WAN analysts. LAN ATM users use the ABR, VBR, CBR designations exclusively.

Let us look at the structure of the ATM cell, to see what the SAR turns the native streams into.

• The ABR or UBR (AAL Class 5) cell has a 5 octet header, with a 48 octet payload.

• The CBR (AAL Class 1) cell has a 5 octet header, with an additional 2 octet SAR header, for a payload of 46 octets. Voice rarely fills up the entire payload, because waiting to fill up a cell can induce delay.

• VBR implementations rarely use their optional SAR header and have a 48 octet payload just like ABR/UBR.

ATM Model

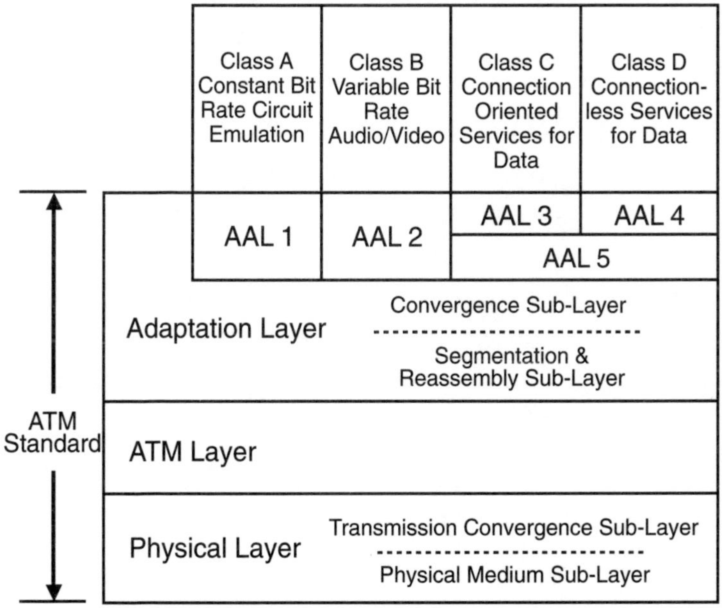
Class A
Constant Bit
Rate Circuit
Emulation
Class B
Variable Bit
Rate
Audio/Video
Class C
Connection
Oriented
Services for
Data
Class D
Connection-
less Services
for Data
AAL 1
AAL 2
AAL 3
AAL 4
AAL 5
Adaptation Layer
Convergence Sub-Layer
Segmentation &
Reassembly Sub-Layer
ATM
Standard
ATM Layer
Physical Layer
Transmission Convergence Sub-Layer
Physical Medium Sub-Layer

Structure of the Cell

The User-Network Interface (**UNI**) and Network-Network Interface (**NNI**), defined by the ATM Forum, define the structure of the ATM cell that follows through each interface. They differ only in the Generic Flow Control (**GFC**) field, which is always filled with 0s. After GFC, we have the **VPI** (Virtual Path Identifier), which names the VPC. The **VCI** (Virtual Channel Identifier) names the VCC.

The Header Checksum, which detects bit errors in the header, is followed by the Payload Type Identifier (**PTI**) and CLP. The PTI indicates whether the cell carries data or network management; it also specifies whether the cell encountered congestion along the way. (The switch will change the PTI to indicate congestion.) These basic cell definitions date back to the birth of ATM; we have developed better ways of dealing with congestion and flow control since then.

The possible PTI values are:

Meaning	Bit Pattern
User-no congestion	000-001
User-congestion	010-011
OAM-segment	100
OAM-end-to-end	101
Reserved	110-111

The use of the PTI field to signal congestion along the path is an example of Explicit Forward Congestion Notification (**EFCI**). FECN in Frame Relay is another example of EFCI.

UNI Cells

<table>
<tr><th>Bit–</th><th>8</th><th>7</th><th>6</th><th>5</th><th>4</th><th>3</th><th>2</th><th>1</th></tr>
<tr><td>Byte 1</td><td colspan="4">GFC</td><td colspan="4">VPI</td></tr>
<tr><td>Byte 2</td><td colspan="4">VPI</td><td colspan="4">VCI</td></tr>
<tr><td>Byte 3</td><td colspan="8">VCI</td></tr>
<tr><td>Byte 4</td><td colspan="4">VCI</td><td colspan="3">PTI</td><td>CLP</td></tr>
<tr><td>Byte 5</td><td colspan="8">HEC</td></tr>
</table>

In the NNI cell, there is no GFC field, so the VPI is 12 bits long.

Operations and Management

OAM means Operations, Administration & Maintenance; some cells are involved in end-to-end management, while others are just testing the segment from switch to switch. One of the PTI values is reserved for RM cells.

Both rate-based and credit-based are examples of what is called **closed loop** congestion control. In an open loop congestion control scheme the network would take unilateral action - throw your traffic out, for example. Throwing your traffic out without feeding back to you that congestion is occurring ("closing the loop") does not allow you to slow down and prevent continuing congestion. Any scheme that closes the loop and allows the sender to take responsive action will give you better overall network performance. Vendors prefer open loop congestion control because it is simpler to engineer.

The Anchorage Accords

Sounds rather like the Paris Peace Talks, doesn't it? The ATM Forum, which has committees developing standards for every aspect of ATM operations, decided to hold a 1996 meeting in which ATM Forum members could make major decisions about the future of this technology. It was decided to allow the various committees to work at their own pace, so the various standards will evolve to new levels independently of each other. This should speed up the standards-development process.

Types of Contracts

Live Voice

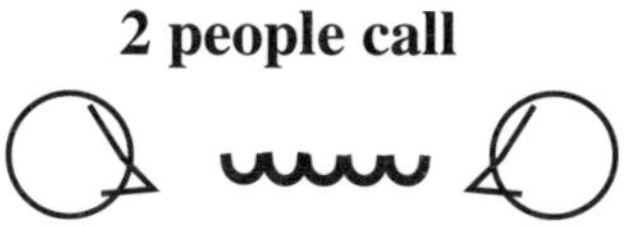

Live Video

Stored Video

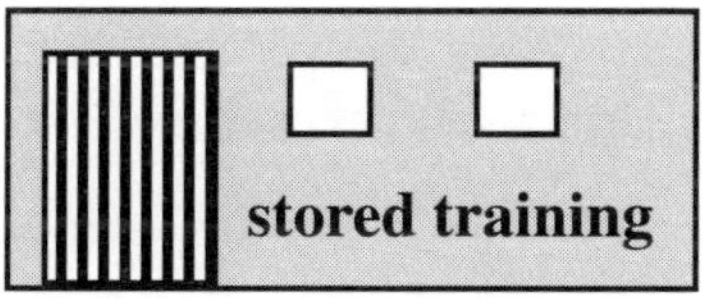

Stored Voice

Data Frames

ATM Layer

The ATM Layer software does the actual VPC/VCC label swapping in the switches, verifies that labels are valid, throws out invalid cells, generates the cell headers, requests valid VCC/VPC numbers from the ATM configuration server (software that can be installed anywhere in the network) and multiplexes cells from multiple VCCs onto a single physical line. This layer also handles ATM signalling.

In an ATM context, **signalling** means the setup, maintenance and clearing of switched virtual circuits (VCCs) through the network. Specific VPs are reserved specifically for use by signalling (which we earlier called control). VP0, VC5 is used for VCC setups, for example.

Multipoint Addressing

Specific VCCs are designated for multipoint transmission. The start of the connection is called the **root** and the various endpoints are **leaves**. When the network gets to the point in the connection setup when it has to **replicate** the cells in order to reach the multiple destinations, we call this a **branch point** and there may be several such on the way to all the leaves. The root usually initiates the multipoint connection, although the latest (4.0) signalling standard allows a **leaf-initiated join** as well. The cells will use a VCC/VPC path number that is assigned to multipoint operations until it reaches a branch point, then the switch will set up individual VCCs to the multiple destinations. Clearly, the standards-makers are botanically-inclined. Many technologies refer to roots, trees, branches and leaves.

Multipoint Connection

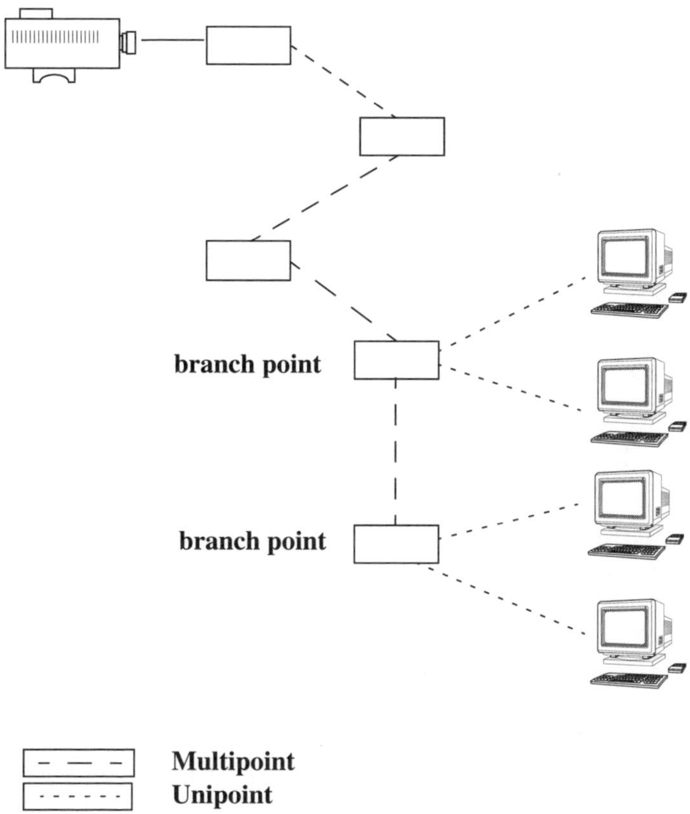

All of our legacy networks depend on multicast and broadcast ability and addresses. In addition, many of the exciting things that we buy ATM to facilitate in our LANs (remote education, tele-medicine) require one-to-many connectivity. This is covered in detail in *Integrating ATM With Legacy LANs*.

Per VC and Per VP Swapping

In a LAN, ABR VCCs are set up and taken down relatively quickly. After all, an ABR VCC represents only the cells that constitute a traditional LAN frame. When a LAN switch swaps VCCs, it is almost always **per-VC** swapping. If you switch by VC, a VCC drops out of one VPC and into the next one, so this is also called **drop-and-insert** (D/I) switching.

In WANs, you can probably imagine how a switch's VPs and VCs might be arranged so all the long-distance telephone traffic coming through Topeka from California en route to Chicago would be put on the same VPs, and then switched **per-VP**. With per-VP swapping, all the VCCs in a particular VPC would be swapped into the same-numbered VCC in the new VPC. Many WAN switches running CBR swap by VP. In addition, WAN switches can swap by VP if all the data traffic on a particular VP is going to the same destination switch (next "hop" on the journey, not necessarily same endpoint).

Project

1. Make a list of all the WAN applications that might use per-VP switching. Describe them in detail.

2. Make a list of all the LAN applications that might use per-VP switching. Describe in detail.

3. Is your ATM installation likely to switch by VP?

VP Switching

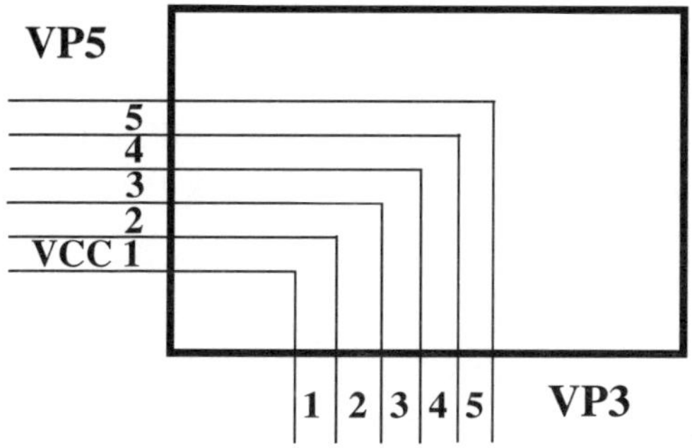

VC Switching within a VP

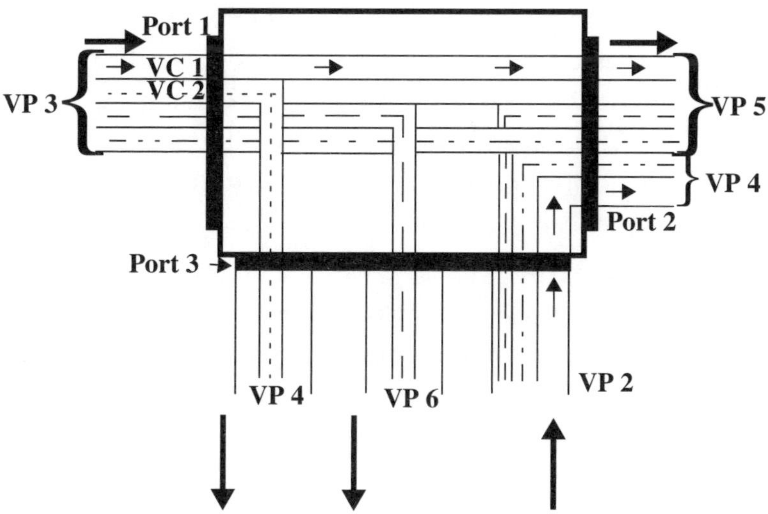

Traffic Management

Traffic management involves access control (coming into the network), congestion in the network (feedback loops between sender and receiver, conformance with the traffic contract, etc.) and minimization of network disruption when cells must be discarded.

The basic form of access control is deciding whether or not to accept the contract, called Connection Admission Control (CAC). Usage Parameter Control (UPC) is action taken at network ingress to verify conformance - the Leaky Bucket, discussed in Chapter 4. UPC is a feature of your WAN provider at the UNI interface, to make sure you aren't getting more bandwidth or service than you paid for!

We can go farther (especially important in WANs!) and actually "shape" the traffic, so that the network gets cells presented to it at precisely the rate (remember **w**?) that it expects on any VCC. Traffic shapers are software entities in the switches that take conforming cells and smooth out the leaky bucket so the interval is always **w**.

Priority Control (the CLP field) tells the network which cells don't pass UPC tests, and can therefore be thrown out if congestion occurs. Flow control prevents or mitigates congestion using either rate-based or credit-based approaches; this matters only to data, since CBR is provisioned at PCR and VBR-rt is almost as well-protected.

Traffic Management Options

- Access Control
  - Connection Access Control (**CAC**)
  - Usage Parameter Control (**UPC**)
- **Traffic Shaping**
- Congestion Control (ABR data)
  - Rate Based (RM cells, Chapter 4)
  - Credit Based (Quantum Flow Control, QFC)
  - Early Packet Discard (**EPD**)
  - Frame Discard (**FD**)
  - Explicit Forward Congestion Indicator (EFCI)
- Error Control
  - Forward Error Connection (FEC)
- Conformance
  - Selective Cell Discard (CLP bit)

Traffic Management for Data Traffic

When dealing with ABR/UBR data flows, we have to consider that all cells are part of higher-layer logical constructs (packets). If we throw out one cell because of an error or a conformance violation, we are wasting bandwidth if we send the rest of the cells that make up the packet; all the cells that follow the lost cell will only be thrown out by the end receiver anyway. One cell lost means an entire packet re-sent. **Early Packet Discard** (EPD) allows us to identify the packet that the lost cell belonged to (the same VCC) and target all other cells in that packet for immediate discard. If we do this, we will eliminate some unnecessary congestion. Other names for this same idea are **Frame Discard** and **Tail Packet Discard**.

Eventually, we would like to have actual correction of bit errors - Forward Error Correction (FEC) - but this is definitely a future idea, well ahead of the industry norm.

Early Packet Discard

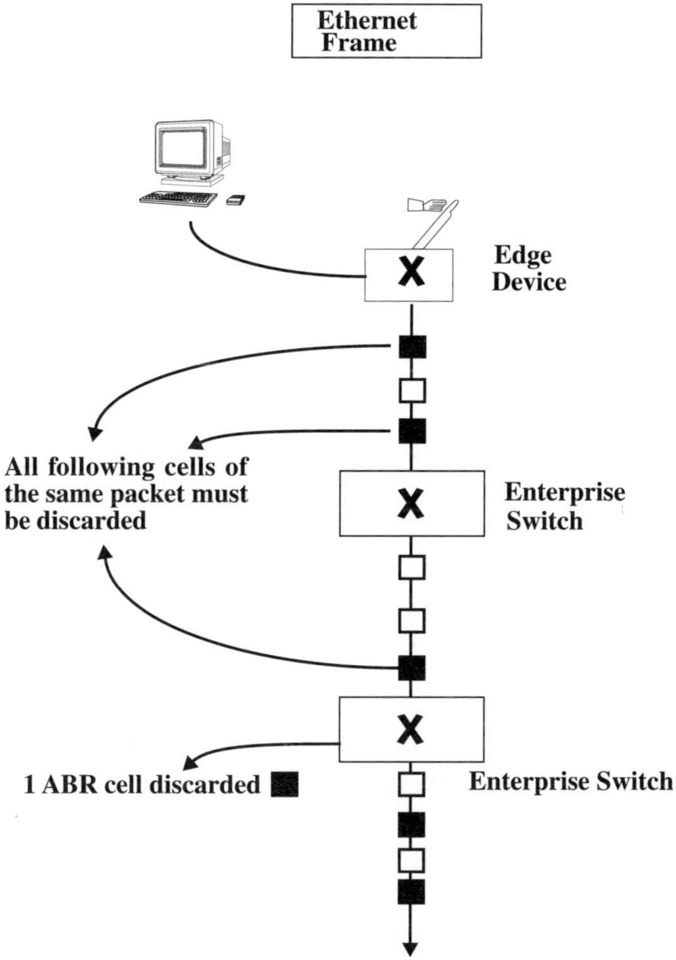

ATM Physical Layer Options

Let's make a transition now to the Physical Layer and look at the various options for bandwidth, and also for NICs, switches and other connection devices.

Some of these specifications are clearly for switch-to-switch or switch to server farm connections; everything over 155.5 falls into this category. The **ATM 25.6** specification and the early **TAXI** (transfer asynchronous transmit/receive interface) spec at 52 Mbps are equally clearly designed for desktops, presumably desktop videoconferencing pioneers. Since one can achieve much more than 25 Mbps to the desktop with Ethernet, and much more cheaply, we do not need to be possessed of psychic powers to predict that sales of 25.6 Mbps NICs have not been sterling.

You can buy ATM NICs from niche vendors and the "usual suspects" (3Com, Bay, etc.). These NICs are available for most server models, as well as other high-performance disk/storage devices. For the actual backbone components themselves, workgroup, backbone and intermediate switches are available from both LAN and WAN vendors.

The existence of an ATM backbone uplink on an Ethernet/Token/Ring switch is common. If an Ethernet switch has an ATM uplink, that means that it converts frames to cells (has SAR software inside it) and is technically an edge device.

Physical Layer Choices

Physical Layer standards are available from the ATM Forum (F) or the ITU (I). The Forum focuses on LANs, while the ITU has focused exclusively on WANs, so some WAN standards are not listed here. Media are Cat 3 and Cat 5 UTP, and multimode (MM) and singlemode (SM) fiber. S (SONET) means the interface provides SONET or SDH framing at the listed rate. For instance, you can run at 155.5 with SONET or without it.

Standard	**Mbps, medium**	**F/I**
ATM 25	25.6, Cat 3	F
TAXI	100, MM	F
TAXI	52.5 (S), Cat 3	F
155.5	155.5 (S), MM	I
155.5	155.5, Cat 5	F
622.5	622.5 (S), MM	F
WAN	DS-1, DS-3	I
WAN	E-1, J-2, E-3	I

In 1997, over a dozen NIC/switch vendors left the market, in some cases because they were bought by a LAN or WAN vendor, in other cases because unsterling sales levels convinced companies not to continue in the ATM marketplace. The existence of Gigabit Ethernet as an option, and the generally high cost of ATM components, is slowing the projected widespread adoption of ATM.

LANE and MPOA

The integrated network will present the edge device with an Ethernet or Token Ring frame. If our network contains non-ATM devices, then we must integrate them with ATM at the MAC Sublayer, and we must also integrate with IP at the Network layer. This means that:

• the Ethernet/Token Ring address has to be mapped to the ATM address, and the frame has to be segmented and re-assembled.

• the edge device has to ask the ATM configuration server (software located somewhere, perhaps in the same box), for VCC/VPC numbers, to create and manage the ATM portion of the journey.

The ATM Forum has developed the LAN Emulation (**LANE**) standard, now in version 2.0, to address the Ethernet to ATM integration question. This standard is in wide use. The Forum also developed the Multiprotocol Over ATM (**MPOA**) standard to integrate IP with ATM. This standard is brand new and integrates with LANE. The existence of proprietary schemes variously called IP Switching, Layer 3 switching and many other things has "muddied" this integration interface with multiple, vendor-specific choices.

These products are the subject of *Integrating ATM With Legacy LANs*, the next book in this series.

Shall We Translate?

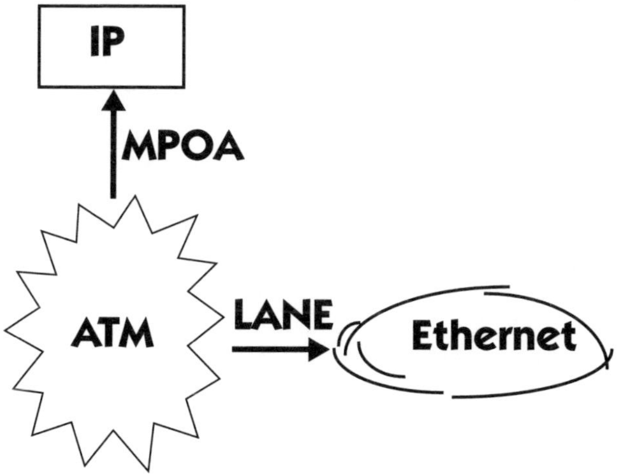

ATM Game Time

Let's call this ATM Jeopardy. You know how to play this: we give you the answers and you give us the questions. (The value of turning the questioning around is that it exercises your brain in a different way.)

1.

   A: 53

2.

   A: 47

3.

   A: 3 bits

4.

   A: It tells you whether the cell is conforming.

5.

   A: 2 octets

6.

   A: Early Packet Discard

7.

   A: Isochronous traffic

8.

   A: They govern flow control.

9.

   A: Resource Management

10.

A: Whether congestion was experienced on the round-trip path.

11

A: It has the strictest traffic contract of all the traffic types.

12.

A: The traffic contract is the least stringent.

13.

A: They must all be of the same type.

14.

A: It's all zeroes.

15.

A: TAXI, 25.6, 155.5 fiber, OC-3

16.

A: Backbones for Token Ring and Ethernet workgroups.

17.

A: GCRA

18.

A: Label-swapping

Make your questions as clear and exact as possible!

ATM Traffic Type Evaluation

For each type of traffic or application listed below, specify which traffic type (CBR, ABR, etc.) the VPI will be a member of. If an application requires 2 VPIs, specify both types.

1. Desktop teleconferencing at the corporate headquarters, as it leaves the desktop
2. Videoconferencing from the corporate video center, coming into the network from the cameras and mikes
3. An Ethernet network, routing into an ATM backbone
4. An FDDI token network, routing into an ATM backbone
5. A Token Ring network, bridging into an ATM backbone
6. A Netware file transfer, coming into the ATM network
7. An email download, coming into the ATM network
8. The initial server signon, transmitted across the ATM network
9. An SNMP poll, transmitted across the ATM backbone
10. A bank ATM query, coming into the ATM network
11. A Websurfer, traversing an ATM segment
12. A doctor, downloading an MRI from a medical database
13. A doctor, demonstrating brain surgery to a colleague at another hospital in realtime

14. Your instructor in her home office, scribbling on a white board and talking about ATM, at the point where her video camera, microphone and Macintosh interface with the Pacific Bell ATM network (which you are also connected to, in a distance learning mode)

15. You and the instructor talking about ATM in a telephone call, via ATM

16. You and your mother, discussing when you're going to get married, quit consulting and get a 'real job', move to Sri Lanka, etc. via ATM

17. Transferring email to your spouse on your home email network which uses, for some inexplicable reason, ATM. Make no assumptions about the sanity of the participants in this network.

18. Transferring email from an Ethernet network to an FDDI Server, across the ATM backbone, at the point where Ethernet joins ATM

19. A telephone call across the ATM backbone, from a user whose data travels on Token Ring

20. Downloading stored video clips across the ATM backbone to your Ethernet segment, at the point where ATM/ Ethernet meet.

Summary

- ATM traffic is assigned to a specific Virtual Channel. Virtual Channels are grouped into Virtual Paths. Switching can be done by Channel or by Path.
- VCs in a VP must be all of the same type (CBR, etc.).
- ATM has Physical layer options from 25.6 Mbps to 1.3 Gbps, on multimode and singlemode fiber as well as Cat 5 UTP.
- ATM uses label-swapping and small VC/VP addresses. Full ATM addresses are resolved into VCs at circuit setup time.
- ATM uses access control, traffic shaping, early packet discard and other methods of traffic management.
- ATM Forum standards for UNI and NNI are evolving rapidly. The Anchorage Accords defined the new UNI 4.0 collection of LAN standards.

Review – Chapter 5

1. What is the VPI field size in NNI? Is it the same for UNI? What is a possible advantage of having more VPs in the network switches compared to edge devices?
2. How big is a Virtual Channel Identifier?
3. How can we get cells across the network with only locally significant VCs?
4. List at least 5 techniques for traffic management in ATM, and define each one's use in the network.
5. What do you think "ingress policing" means? Why?
6. What town hosted the latest standards peace-making effort? Guess which season of the year the meetings were held in.
7. Draw a picture of what happens in an ATM switch when 3 VCs in a CBR VP must swap and all the VCs in an ABR VP must swap.
8. Draw a picture of the UNI cell, labelling and explaining each field. How does the NNI cell differ from this?
9. Explain the functions of LANE and MPOA.
10. (T/F) Quantum Flow Control controls photon torpedoes.
11. Exactly how does Early Packet Discard improve throughput for data traffic? Is it related to Early Token Release?
12. How does ATM provide multicast services to a LAN? What kinds of applications need multicast services?
13. (T/F) Cell Loss Priority gives voice priority over data.
14. ______________ can occur many times along a path from a multicast sender to the various receivers.

Key Words

The words and phrases highlighted in **bold** represent key concepts in this chapter. Please take the time now to write down your own definitions of these terms, using the list below and additional paper if needed. Then compare your efforts to the training text. This is an excellent way for you to determine weak points in the breadth and depth of your understanding of this chapter.

VCC	**Data VCC**
VCI	**Control VCC**
VPC	**Root/leaf**
VPI	**Join**
locally-significant	**CAC**
label-swapping	**UNI**
Tail Packet Discard	**NNI**
Early Packet Discard	**OAM**
LANE	**signalling**
MPOA	**replicate**
drop-and-insert	**branch point**
Frame Discard	**closed loop**
UPC	**EFCI**
Traffic Shaping	**PTI**
GFC	**Adaptation Layer**
SAR	**globally-significant**
per-VC swap	**per-VP swap**
TAXI	**ATM25.6**

6
Let's Compare

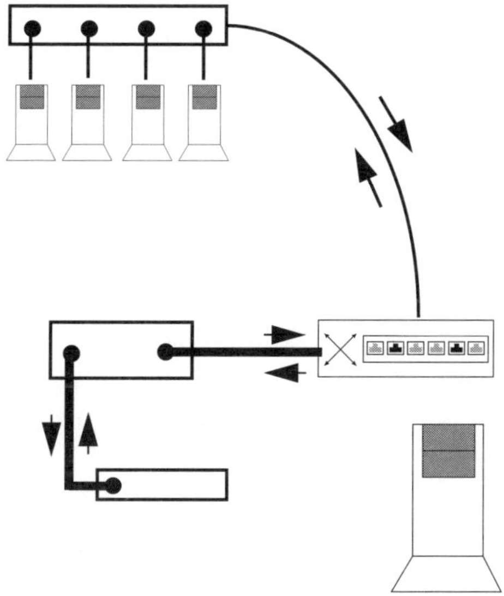

Goals of this Chapter

When you complete this chapter, you should be able to:

- ❐ Decide if and where to use ATM in your network
- ❐ Decide if and where to use Gigabit Ethernet in your network
- ❐ Decide if and where to use Ethernet, Token Ring, FDDI or Fast Token Ring switching, and other less common choices, in your network

All the Facts, Ma'am

Let's keep in mind that an upgrade to switching from hubbing, or the adoption of something other than ATM and Gigabit Ethernet, could be your most sensible decision. What are your "other" choices?

FDDI Anyone?

You can, if your bandwidth numbers allow, choose to put switched half-duplex or full-duplex FDDI in your backbone. This choice appeals to network managers and CIOs who prefer a technology choice with enough history that its foibles are known and experienced support staff can be hired.

It is possible, though highly exotic, to put SONET under FDDI and bump its speed into the 622.5 Mbps range. SONET replaces the FDDI PHY and PMD specifications.

Fast Token Ring

Until 1997, it was a given that ATM was the only evolution path for Token Ring users who were outgrowing 16 Mbps switching. However, the Fast Token Ring Alliance is busy creating a 100 Mbps upgrade. It must be said that all the major Token Ring vendors are supporting this effort (at least verbally). Token Ring buyers now have more choices.

Fibre Channel

This technology is an excellent choice for disk farms and related data storage devices. Because storage I/O is a limiting factor in distributed environments, you could give your overall network performance a major boost with judicious implementation of Fibre Channel in your disk farms and server farms. With multigigabit speeds and a long standards history, this is an excellent technology choice for your backend storage needs.

Making Choices

In this chapter we will look at all the information of the previous chapters and apply that knowledge to your network. The place to start is the obvious question: what problem are you trying to solve with a new technology?

We will look at the following issues, compare them for the two technologies and then create decision matrices:

- Speed
- Applications
- Integration with existing LANs
- WAN interfaces
- Long-term, comprehensive cost factors
- Future planning

In order to accomplish this chapter's analysis, please have your work from Chapter 1 spread in front of you as you work your way through this chapter.

Speed

Are you running out of bandwidth in the backbone? In the server farm? Both Gigabit Ethernet and ATM can give you a fast Physical Layer, although GEnet has an edge here: all switch interfaces are full-duplex.

Both technologies are available on optical fiber and on Cat.5 UTP.

Medium Dependency	
GE	**ATM**
Fiber	All Media
Cat 5 @ 25m. only	

Applications

The "problematical" application, of course, is videoconferencing, both room-size systems and desktop videoconferencing.

It is obvious what ATM can do for isochronous traffic.

What can Gigabit Ethernet do for those potential buyers who want to run room videoconferencing systems or desktop videoconferencing over the data network? So, will Gigabit Ethernet give you acceptable performance for all the types of isochronous traffic? In a word, yes. It has been clearly demonstrated in numerous tests that Ethernet can provide adequate highways for voice and video provided that no congestion occurs.

If you use GEnet for your isochronous traffic, you have to really manage your network, monitoring peak traffic levels and ensuring that congestion never occurs. Most of us won't/can't do this. With close to 1000 Mbps, it is hard to imagine congestion being a problem, isn't it? However, we all know that our users will find things to with the bandwidth we give them. One of the things they will do is videoconference.

It is worth noting that the entire world of data is evolving to accommodate isochronous needs. We have a new IPv6 header, plus an optional isochronous support header. IP routers and switches are announced every day with one scheme or another for giving iso-traffic the right-of-way it needs to survive in Ethernet networks. Isochronous traffic support is not a simply Data Link Layer issue any more.

Let's ask some questions, to help put the ATM/GEnet question in perspective:

• 1) How much isochronous traffic does your worst-case plan show?

• 2) Is it on the backbone or into the server farms (the most congested sections), in other congested locations or in specific departments?

• 3) How soon will the isochronous avalanche arrive?

• 4) Why do you want to integrate the isochronous traffic? (If your videoconferencing goes straight from a single room system to a WAN connection, you may spend less money with a non-ATM installation. Look at the cost section.)

WAN Interfaces

Your pre-choice of a WAN technology can help you in the LAN backbone choice. If you anticipate a significant amount of ATM WAN traffic, it makes sense to have an ATM LAN backbone. Most people choose the LAN first, then let the WAN choice derive from it, but in your network, the WAN decision may be more strategic.

Connection to WANs from LAN	
GE Backbone	**ATM Backbone**
• No standards work done yet, too new	• LAN/WAN using same technology
• Edge devices to WAN deal with the familiar Ethernet frame	• Other interfaces uncertain
	• Integration with ATM WANs may not be seamless

If you are doing a lot of WAN videoconferencing, and are already using ATM for that, it might tilt your LAN decision, since your staff already has a lot of ATM technical experience.

Integration with Existing LANs

There is no doubt that the existence of Gigabit Ethernet should be a significant factor for any network manager who has an existing Ethernet installation. With the same frame, you can have a backbone devoid of the translation problems of LANE/MPOA/etc. as you attempt to integrate Ethernet, IP and ATM.

IP already has existing and well-known integration between itself and Ethernet, which the added speed of GEnet will not change.

If you choose Gigabit Ethernet, you have a chance to leverage existing expertise in your staff - with respect to the Ethernet interface to other software. Gigabit Ethernet hardware itself will require new education, of course. The applications that run on your network will not be disrupted by the Physical Layer changes of moving from Fast Ethernet to Gigabit Ethernet.

Long-term Comprehensive Costs

This is the section where we look at ALL the costs associated with ALL the decisions you can possibly make. Have a sobering cup of coffee, and write down a realistic number. Then double it. THAT's realistic.

Some items are universal:

• Retraining costs tuition, lost time from work and temp help. If you try to "save money" by expecting your staff to do their regular job AND retrain, the joke is on you: they can't do either effectively. You are wasting your tuition money if you don't give your staff release time to learn. People who are overworked will start job-hunting. In addition, you will end up with tired people running the network, making stupid mistakes and creating more trouble. And, of course, you will roll out your new technology with staff who don't know what they're doing. Calculate the real costs of retraining.

• New technologies require new tools. Sorry, this rule is eternal and cannot be broken.

• Adding new vendors to the mix will give you an added 20% in your ongoing operations costs, due to interoperability fun. Is the new vendor/technology going to lower your existing costs or improve your billable throughput more than 20%?

Now let's look at some specific factors in choosing ATM or Gigabit Ethernet.

Gigabit Ethernet: Cost Issues

• Initial hardware costs are high.

• It's barely defined, much less adequately tested. Elsewhere in this chapter there is a chart that asks you how you feel about doing a vendor's beta test for them - on your corporate-critical network.

• You only have to retrain your staff on the specifics of Gigabit hardware and software. They can accomplish this in a week of intensive training.

Table 1: Cost Worksheet

Factor	Cost (+/-)
Base hardware	
Retraining	
Retrofit of existing equipment possible?	
Downtime Costs	
New tools	
Cost savings (compared to current ops costs)	

ATM: Cost Issues

• If you add ATM to the network, plan on at least 3 months full time retraining time just to get your staff basically savvy. You will need additional time for your staff to get up to speed on the new analysis, monitoring and test tools. That time has to be full-time, with hands-on practice included. If you train some people and not others, inevitably the savvy ones will all be on vacation, sick leave and business trips when your crisis occurs.

• To get speeds comparable to Gigabit Ethernet, you need ATM on OC-12 or higher. Does your vendor have such interfaces? How old are they (have they been on the market more than 6 months)? If your OC-12 implementation is as new as GEnet hardware, ATM's advantage as the more stable solution disappears.

• One of ATM's great strengths is that its support for all traffic types is built into the basic design. You do not have to worry about voice/video performance degrading as the network becomes busier - a distinct possibility with GEnet.

Videoconference: ATM?

Consider the costs and other factors associated with a sepa-

Factor	Cost
Videoconference hardware	
Added software	
Test and other tools	
Line costs (DS-1, DS-3, etc.)	
Staff training	
Interactivity for the users (do you need a full return link?)	
Associated PC interfaces, faxes, etc.	

rate videoconference network. You might spend less if you don't insist on putting your videoconference traffic on your

LAN backbone. Be honest; be comprehensive. The latest video standards create traffic that can be fed into an ATM network, so your non-ATM videoconference network could feed into a later ATM implementation.

Downtime Costs

The chart below will remind you that the final component of your decision is your specific network's tolerance for brand-new technologies. You need to calculate the cost of downtime associated with a particular choice, if the technologies are not equally reliable. How do you do it? At this point, read the trade press for independent lab tests of equipment, and carefully read and evaluate the test design before you believe any test results.

Your Risk/Stress Tolerance

	GEnet	ATM
Newness	Barely Newborn	New
Cost of Equipment	Pretty High	High but Declining
Cost of Retraining Staff	GE details only	Complete retraining

Your Risk/Stress Tolerance		
Reliability of Equipment	Barely beta-tested!	Laughably low, but out for years
Support for ISO as Traffic Levels Increase	Relies on over-provisioning, so keep an eye on utilization levels	Always protects ISO traffic regardless of congestion
Complexity	Less	More

In the table above, ISO stands for isochronous traffic.

Final Matrix

In this final matrix, you pull together all the factors in your decision. You can look at time that a transition will cost you (take your staff away from other issues) as another issue in addition to the $cost of the time lost.

Table 2: Final Matrix

	GEnet	ATM	Other
Speeds			
Applications			
WAN?			

Table 2: Final Matrix

	GEnet	ATM	Other
Upgrade costs (transfer from other table)			
Time (not cost) associated with this choice			
Integration costs (existing LANs)			
Interops, new vendor or product			
Tools needed			
Your issues:			

As your Chapter 1 analysis showed, you have different problems and needs in different places in the network. This matrix may show you that you need a specific solution in one part of your network, and another solution elsewhere. Remember, however, that one of your goals was to reduce complexity and multi-protocol hassles in your network by reducing the number of technologies that you are supporting!

Products and Vendors

As the Product Availability chart shows, ATM has been shipping products for several years and the market is somewhat stable. Most GEnet vendors are concentrating on repeater and switch development; NICs seem less of a priority.

We are primarily considering Gigabit Ethernet as a full-duplex switch-to-switch link for the backbone. NICs become more important as adopters start migrating Gigabit Ethernet to the server farm, and to high-speed disk farms. We expect GEnet to impact the HPPI and HSSI markets.

Product Availability

GE	ATM
NICs	NICs
Full Duplex Switches	Switches
	Edge Devices
	LANE, MPOA, etc.

The Usual Suspects (3Com, Cisco, Bay, Cabletron, Xylan, Digital, HP, IBM, Intel, etc.) are offering GEnet as uplinks on existing hubs/switches/routers, as well as selling enterprise (backbone) switches and NICs. Most of the Usual Suspects are also ATM vendors, an unenviable position for a sales rep without clear sales differentiators. You will fare better in discussions if YOU know what you need, and what the issues are.

ATM Standards Checklist

ATM Standard	Needed in your network?
UNI	Yes
NNI	
PNNI	
LANE	If you have Ethernet
MPOA	Recommended
RM	Yes
Others?	

Future Planning

Now that you have analyzed what you need for your network right now, and have probably developed a good feel for what your decision is going to be, it's time for us to throw a monkey-wrench or adjustable spanner into the decision mechanism.

Consider what you are likely to need in 5 years, with respect to:

- speeds,
- applications, including isochronous support, and
- integration of infrastructures.

In some cases, you may know that new technologies and applications are in your future. For instance, you might have concluded that you don't need ATM because Gigabit Ethernet can handle your isochronous traffic needs well. What if you know that the organization has decided that ATM is the ultimate strategic technology for the 21st Century? If that is true, you might want to adopt ATM as your backbone now, using the next 5 years to build staff expertise in this new technology. On the other hand, you could install Gigabit Ethernet and prove how wonderful it is, hoping that this might reverse the organizational mandate.

You should consider what your applications mix will be in 5 years. More client/server applications means more backbone bandwidth. An increased reliance on videoconferencing to reduce overall travel costs (in dollars and time) could suggest an ATM backbone in your future.

You may be surprised at the results of your analysis. You may decide to postpone adoption of any adventurous new technologies for another 6-12 months. You may decide that you have to retool your upgrade plan. You may also find yourself confirmed in your original plan. In any case, knowledge is power.

We are extremely enthusiastic about the future of all the technologies examined in this book. You may consider any of them strategic to your corporate information highway, with no fear that any of them with be a "flash in the pan", even the currently over-hyped ones.

Additional discussion of the Ethernet/ATM interface, and the cost issues associated with this edge translation are contained in *Integrating ATM with Legacy LANs*, in this series.

Appendix

Details, Resources, Sources & Answers

This Appendix contains additional technical details that a network manager may not need to know (needs vary, just as networks do), as well as some sources of additional information. for your continued study. It also contains the answers to the review questions.

Section 1: Additional Technical Details on ATM

In this section, you can see some additional technical details that were omitted from Chapters 4 and 5. Many of these issues are explored in detail in *Integrating ATM With Legacy LANs.*

Private/Public Network to Network Interface (PNNI)

Normal setup operations cannot cope with creating paths through potentially thousands of ATM switches, from sender to receiver. The PNNI protocol is sometimes called "ATM routing," a misnomer since a MAC protocol can't route. However, it does allow switches to accurately and rapidly choose appropriate paths for call establishment. It is currently not implemented widely (some vendors prefer their proprietary algorithms; others just don't visualize networks large enough to need this).

Signalling

In an ATM context, **signalling** means the setup, maintenance and clearing of switched virtual circuits (VCCs) through the network. The 4 subsections of signalling in the ATM Forum specs are: Call Establishment, Call Status, Call Clearing and Point-to-Multipoint operations. The process of call setup has already been discussed in general. Specific VPs are set up specifically for use by signalling. VP0, VC5 is used for call setup, for example.

Quality of Service

In the UNI 4.0 standard, cell loss ratio, peak-to-peak cell delay variation and maximum cell transfer delay are required parts of the QOS calculation. Cell error ratio, severely errored cell block ratio and cell misinsertion rate are optional.

Section 2: Resources

1. Organizations

The Institute of Electrical and Electronics Engineers (IEEE)
345 E. 47th Street
New York, NY 10017
USA

International Organization for Standardization (ISO)
Case Postale 56
CH-1211 Geneve 20
Switzerland

For more information on ATM, you don't have to contact the ITU; contact the **ATM Forum** at:

ATM Forum
2570 W. El Camino Real, Suite 304
Mountain View, CA 94040
USA

Tel: 650-949-6700
Fax: 650-949-6705
info@atmforum.org
http://www.atmforum.com

The Forum publishes a regular newsletter, appropriately titled *53 Bytes*

The **Gigabit Ethernet Alliance**, a newly-formed organization, will provide you with the latest information on vendors supporting this new technology as well as other information. There are over 50 members of this alliance, and membership is growing.

www.gigabit-ethernet.com

2. Publications

If you are not already receiving these publications, call and request a sample copy or visit your local technical bookstore:

1. Communications Week (weekly news)
Manhasset, NY (516) 562-5530

2. Network World (weekly news)
Framingham, MA (508) 875-6400

www.nwfusion.com includes online access to articles.

3. Business Communications Review
Hinsdale, IL (800) 227-1234

3. More on Standards

The ANSI/IEEE 802.3 CSMA/CD LAN standard has many subsections including the new 802.3z **Gigabit Ethernet** versions. These standards are the most accessible, both in readability and availability in bookstores. It corresponds to ISO 8802-3.

Answer Key

The questions that require analysis of your network, or which have complex answers, are omitted, so you can discuss these in your training program. Enjoy!

Chapter 2

1. hub
2. cut-thru and store/forward
4. No collisions, short IFG
5. yes
6. Unless its full-duplex
7. Switches and NICs
12. No

Chapter 3

1. No. All wires already in use for signalling.
2. Manchester. It's already known and can handle 100 Mbps.
7. Overprovision, so congestion is never a factor.
9. Videoconferencing.
11. Of course not.
12. No. 62% of all USA networks.

Chapter 4

1. ABR, CBR, VBR-rt, VBR-nrt, UBR

9. ATM and AAL, perhaps Physical (it depends)

10. 2; 2; CBR and VBR-rt

11. Use of PCR, vs MCR and SCR

13. Jitter

14. CBR.

16. CDVT

Chapter 5

1. 1.5 octets; no

6. Anchorage. Not winter!

9. LANE translates Ethernet to ATM. MPOA interfaces IP to ATM.

10. No.

11. It throws away cells that will get thrown away at the source. No.

13. No.

14. Replication

Glossary

Welcome to the comprehensive High-Speed Networking Glossary. This glossary is composed of your Key Words as well as several hundred additional words from the High-Speed LAN and WAN marketplace - ATM, SONET/SDH, SMDS, Frame Relay, SS7, ISDN - as well as T/E-carrier and general networking. Your **Key Words** are left blank, so you can fill in with the definitions you created as you worked your way through the text. Other words that are left blank are Key Words in the advanced ATM text *Integrating ATM With Legacy Networks*, which you are encouraged to add to your collection.

This Glossary is also available (with all the words filled in, of course) in disk form, for site licensing. Put the Glossary on your computer or server and consult it easily whenever you encounter an unfamiliar term! See the Order Form in the back of this book.

Numerics

10base	One of the 802.3 versions.
100base	Fast Ethernet version.
1000base	Gigabit Ethernet

	For the 3 above, FX is the fiber version. TX uses 2 pairs of Cat 5 wire.
802	IEEE committee whose subcommittees create LAN standards

A

A	A bit in T-1 Extended superframe (24 frames) and standard superframe (12 frames) use the A bit for signaling. This is one of 2 bits in superframe and 4 bits in extended superframe that are "robbed" from the data. Robbed bits are always in the LSB position. See also SF and ESF.
A	A bytes in SONET The A bytes are located in SOH and are concerned with frame alignment so they are the first bytes in the header.
AAL	ATM Adaptation Layer This is the uppermost layer of the ATM model with 5 different types. Each AAL accepts a different kind of incoming bit stream and passes it on to the SAR. AAL1 accepts constant bit rate circuit-switched input. Type 2 accepts variable bit rate circuit-switched input. Type 5 is for data and types 3/4 have been abandoned.
ABR	Available Bit Rate Your definition:
ADCCP	Advanced Data Communications Control Procedure A Data Link protocol, created by ANSI, and very similar to HDLC.
ADM	Add/Drop Multiplexor (SONET/SDH) A multiplexor with 2 or more incoming data streams, at

	least one of which is being added or dropped from the SPE.
ADPCM	Adaptive Differential Pulse Code Modulation A form of analog to digital coding.
AMI	Alternate Mark Inversion AMI is the older form of line coding for T-1 in North America. Mark is the 1 signal, compared to space for the 0. In order to allow T-1 muxes to pass not only 1s and 0s but also clocking information (keep their clocks synchronized), the mark goes positive for the first mark, negative for the next mark etc. Voltage that stays high or low signifies a space. The reason T-1 systems need a certain 1s density, and have to add (stuff) a mark if it doesn't occur naturally, is because only a mark will change the voltage. If you don't have a mark often enough to resync the clocks, your clocks may drift and begin misframing the data. See also NRZI.
ANI	Automatic Number Identification This is an ISDN feature, relying on the Signaling System 7 infrastructure, that relays to the called party the phone number of the calling party. This option is very controversial.
ANM	Answer Message In Signaling System 7, ANM is the signal that the called party returns to the caller to indicate that a connection has been achieved.
ANSI	American National Standards Institute This is a U.S. standards creation organization that exports its work to ISO and the ITU/TSS. ANSI standard numbers start with a letter followed by numbers, as in X1T1.
ASI	Alternate Space Inversion ASI is the opposite of AMI. Spaces change polarity.
ATM	Asynchronous Transfer Mode ATM is a Data Link technology that requires a high-speed

	physical fabric below it. It can carry both circuit and packet-switched data in standard 53 octet cells.
AU	Administrative Unit In SDH, this is the payload plus its pointers. SDH likes to use AUs as units for discussion because these are the units that are multiplexed and demultiplexed when moving to higher speed levels.
AUG	Administrative Unit Group One or more AUs.
AUI	Attachment Unit Interface The AUI is a physical connection between a user desktop and the network in a thick coax LAN.
AWG	American Wire Gauge This measures the wire size, for your wiring infrastructure.

B

B	B bit for T-1 Extended superframe (24 frames) and standard superframe (12 frames) use the B bit for signaling. This is one of 2 bits in superframe and 4 bits in extended superframe that are "robbed" from the data. Robbed bits are always in the LSB position. See also SF and ESF.
B	B bytes in SONET There is one B byte in SOH and one in LOH. Both are concerned with error monitoring.
B	Bearer Channel Bearer channels in ISDN carry user data, in 64 Kbps DS-0s. In BRI, there are 2 B channels, while in PRI, there are 23 B channels. These numbers refer to North America. In countries that use the E-1 standard, PRI = 30 B channels. B channels can carry voice, video or data.

B8ZS	Binary 8 Zero Substitution This is a coding scheme to prevent sender and receiver from becoming unsynchronized if the data stream contains too many 0s (and therefore no clocking information). This scheme prevents 8 0s from occurring in a row, to maintain 1s density during transmission. The receiving mux strips the coding and recreates the 8 0s. See ZBTSI.
BART	Bay Area Rapid Transit A great way to get to meetings in the SF Bay area.
BASize	Buffer Allocation Size This field in the SMDS header tells the receiver how many octets the PDU will require when it is buffered. The trailer has a 2 octet length field that conveys the same information. This equals the total length of the PDU, including header/trailer and information.
BCD	Binary Coded Decimal The decimal numbers (0–9), expressed in binary form, used for the SMDS address.
BECN	Backward Explicit Correction Notification BECN is a field in the frame relay header that a congested node can use to alert other nodes that it is experiencing congestion on a certain virtual circuit (called a DLCI). As a method of flow control, this is pretty primitive. The Frame Relay Forum is working to standardize the more powerful approaches that various vendors are working on.
BER	Basic Encoding Rules The BER for a technology defines how characters are encoded into digital bits.
BER	Bit Error Rate The number of bit errors allowed in SONET and ATM is very low. You can expect no more than 1 bit error for every 10^{11} bits transmitted.

BERT	BER Tester BERT tests bit errors. Equipment and technologies advertise their extremely low BERs.
BES	Bursty Errored Second Up to 319 CRC errors in extended superframe framing. An errored second is a second of transmission time in which an error occurred on the transmission line.
BETag	Beginning/End Tag This is one of the fields in the SMDS header. The sequence number allows the receiver to take the information field, add it to the information field in another cell with the next sequence number (and so on) and reassemble the original user frame.
BIB	Backward Indicator Bit The BIB is a field in the Signalling System 7 signaling unit (SU).
B-ICI	Broadband Intercarrier Interface Your definition:
BIP	Bit Interleaved Parity BIP is a generic name for an error checking method. SONET uses BIP 8, for example.
B-ISDN	Broadband ISDN Broadband ISDN is a model and associated protocols and services that can take business and individual subscribers well into the 21st century. B-ISDN includes ATM as well as new services above the ATM Data Link cell switching service. B-ISDN channels, since they begin at 100 Mbps and extend through the gigabit range, will be able to incorporate all our existing services.
bit sync	Bit synchronous VT1.5 In bit sync mapping of the T1 frame into a VT, the frame does not align with the VT. You specify this mode by

setting the first 2 bits of the S octet to 10. See byte sync, VT.

BNC — Bayonet Navy Connector

There are a whole series of BNC connectors for various interfaces in the data comm area, including T-1 and premises networks. The connector standards define the shape of the connector, the pin placements, etc. Guess who developed this standard?

BNS — Broadband Network Switch

This word refers to any broadband switch, but usually involves ATM and Broadband ISDN. The minimum speed is generally DS-3 (45 Mbps) or OC-1 (52 Mbps).

BOM — Beginning Of Message

When an SMDS message is divided into cells, the first cell gets the BOM designation, the last one is the End Of Message (EOM) and the middle ones are all tagged Continuation Of Message (COM). The receiving switch uses the BOM, COM and EOM to reassemble the cells into the original frame. The SegT (segment type) field of the L2-PDU is 10 for BOM.

BPDU — Bridge Protocol Data Unit

Bridges following the spanning tree protocol use BPDUs to communicate with each other.

BPV — Bipolar Violation

Two marks in the same polarity in a row is a bipolar violation. A particular pattern of bipolar violations is used to indicate framing conditions (as opposed to data) in T-1.

BRA — Basic Rate Access

BRA is the basic ISDN 2B+D service worldwide. Each B channel is 64 Kbps and the D for signaling is 16 Kbps. See also PRA.

BRI — Basic Rate Interface

BRI is the interface specification for BRA

bridge	You define:
BRT	Broadband Remote Terminal A BRT is a high-speed broadband device (access node) that feeds into ATM, SONET or SMDS, depending on what layer it operates at. Most BRTs operate at DS-3, OC-1 or higher rates.
BSN	Backward Sequence Number In ISDN's Signaling System 7, BSN is the sequence number of the signaling unit that's expected to arrive next.
BSS	Broadband Switching System The BSS is a central office switch that switches cells for ATM.
burst	Exceed a parameter In Frame Relay, exceed the CIR; in SMDS, exceed the SIR and in ATM, to send at PCR. And (you add):
BUS	Broadcast & Unknown Server The BUS, part of LANE, handles broadcast frames and frames whose ATM address is unknown. Your definition:
Byte Sync	Byte synchronous VT1.5 In this option, the T1 frame is aligned with the VT. The S octet is available for signaling. The FDL carried by the F bits are in the S octet. This mode is advantageous compared to bit sync because it wastes less overhead and allows customers to preserve more control information.

C, D, E

C	C bits in ESF The 6 C bits in ESF provide a CRC. These C bits are part of the signaling (robbed bits).
C	C bytes in SONET The C bytes provide names and labels and are located in SOH and POH.
CAC	 Your definition:
CBR	Constant Bit Rate Your definition:
CCIS 6	Common Channel Interoffice Signaling System 6 Commonly known as Signaling System 6, this scheme is the predecessor of Signaling System 7, used with ISDN. Both CCS6 and CCS7 use out-of-band signaling.
CCITT	Comité Consultativ International de Télégraphique et Téléphonique The old name for what is now the TSS. The ITU/TSS is part of the International Telecommunications Union (ITU), which is part of the United Nations.
CCR	 Your definition:
CCS 7	Common Channel Signaling System 7 CCS7 is the signaling substructure of ISDN. It carries the control information to control, bill, recover from errors etc. This is the long distance continuation of the local D channels in ISDN.

CD

Your definition:

CDR

Your definition:

CDV Cell Delay Variation

Your definition:

CDVT Cell Delay Variation Tolerance

Your definition:

cell An ATM frame

CEPT Conférence European de Poste et Téléphone
This European standards creation organization created many standards in the 80s, but ETSI does most European standards development today.

CER Cell Error Rate

Your definition:

CIR Committed Information Rate

In frame relay networks, each access device has a committed information rate that represents its contractual traffic level. Networks differ in how they treat traffic over the CIR: automatically throw it out, tag it for disposal if congestion occurs (to ensure fairness of access) or simply allow it to pass without taking action. Allowing an access device to substantially exceed the CIR is referred to as bursting and a public frame relay network will advertise its burst capacity and how it bills for bursts.

CL Connectionless

A form of network service in which a connection is not set up prior to sending data. LLCs, Network Layer Service and other network entities may be connectionless.

Class You define:

CLID Calling Line Identification

Just another name for ANI.

CLIP Calling Line Identification Presentation

This is a customer premises service that allows you to support CLID. In a non-ISDN phone, this could include a separate display for showing the number.

CLIR Calling Line Identification Restriction

This is a customer premises service that prevents the display of incoming number information and the outgoing delivery of information. See CLID and CLIP.

CLNP Connectionless Network Protocol

The OSI-standard datagram protocol. IP is an example of a datagram network protocol.

CLNS Connectionless Network Service

CLNS is the network service that CLNP (the protocol) delivers.

Clock The synchronizing element

Synchronous networks like SONET need to keep every element in the network synchronized, that is, expecting specific actions at specific times. To do this, each element needs a clock. See stratum.

CLP Cell Loss Priority

CLP, one of the fields in the ATM header, indicates whether the cell is legal - whether it fits its traffic contract.

CLR — Cell Loss Rate

Your definition:

CMI — Coded Mark Inversion

CMI is the line signaling for STS-3 at 45 Mbps.

CMI — Constant Mark Inverted

This CMI is the line coding for the T-1 local loop interface in Japan. Japan is the only nation outside of North America that uses T-1 instead of E-1. See also J2.

CMR

Your definition:

codec — coder/decoder

A codec converts an analog signal into a digital signal for wide-area (video) transmission, and back again. Some people call codecs "modems for video."

COFA — Change of Frame Alignment

When the synchronous payload envelope (SPE) moves within a STS frame, you have a COFA. The H bits indicate where the SPE is in the field.

collision domain — You define:

COM — Continuation of Message

This COM field tells the receiving mux that the cell is part of an ongoing message reconstruction from a higher level frame. See BOM.

CONS — Connection Oriented Network Service

CONS is the opposite of CLNS, offering virtual circuits in contrast to datagrams; TCP is CONS. Isochronous traffic requires CONS.

payload — The ITU uses this term to describe what a payload gets

	placed in. See SPE.
congestion management	Your definition:
Converge	Converge is the word used for the process of connecting one technology type to the technology that implements functions at the layer immediately above or below it. For instance, we talk about the convergence function between SONET and ATM or IP and ATM.
CP	Customer Premises Everything that the telephone company doesn't own is probably some customer's property. The interface between the local loop and CP is generally a critical one, where conversions occur.
CPCS	Common Part Convergence Sublayer The CPCS is the bottom-most layer of the Convergence Sublayer in ATM and is concerned with error detection. As the name implies, this sublayer contains the common functions for all the traffic types. See SSCS.
CPN	Customer Premises Node A customer premises (CP) node is a switch that resides on the customer's premises rather than the telephone company's. As networks become more sophisticated and vendors offer ATM premises equipment, more of the packet conversion function will be moved to CP.
credit-based	A form of congestion management in ATM See also QFC, rate based. Your definition:
CRC	Cyclic Redundancy Checking Detects bit errors in frames.

CRV Coding Rule Violation

In order to allow the receiver to know which bit is the F bit in STS format, the sender uses a unique bit signal for the F bit. The special signal violates the coding rule.

CS Convergence Sublayer

In SMDS, the convergence sublayer adds a header and trailer before passing the frame over the DXI interface to be fragmented into cells.

CSMA/CD Carrier Sense, Multiple Access, Collision Detect

CSMA is contention access in a local area network, used in Ethernet, 802.3 and similar LANs. Other LANs share multiple access with token passing.

CSI Convergence Sublayer Indication

The CSI field in the SAR-PDU header in AAL 1 carries RTS. As always, an "indication" refers to control signalling information.

CSU Channel Service Unit

The CSU used to be part of the CO but over the past two decades this device has migrated to CP. The CSU provides an interface between a DSU or T-1 mux and the CO local loop. A CSU provides the interface to the T-1 signaling.

cut-through A switch that (you complete):

CV Coding Violation

The CV indicates an error in a SONET transmission.

D D bit in VT1.5

The D bit is one of 4 signaling bits in the VT1.5 in locked mode (SONET). This bit is part of the S octet.

D D bits in ES

In extended superframe, the D bits are half the overhead in the framing (F) position, so they occur in alternate F bits. The D bits act as the facilities data link (FDL). D bits

	have nothing to do with the D signaling bits in each DS-0 of frame numbers 18 & 24 of ESF.
D	D bits in SONET If a frame needs to slip back one octet, and the H3 position will be filled with data, the D (decrement) bits in the preceding H pointers are inverted (1 to 0 or 0 to 1). These decrement bits alert the receiver to the fact that the SPE has slipped back one octet. See I bits, float, SPE and H octets.
D	D Channel The D channel is 16 Kbps in BRA and 64 Kbps in PRA (ISDN). The D channels are used for signaling–the out-of-band signaling that ISDN is famous for. SS 7 is the wide-area continuation of the D channels. You can also multiplex some user data on the D channels since they are packet-switched.
D4	D4 Format for T-1 The D4 format for T-1 defines framing. Bits are either signaling or payload.
D/I	Drop and Insert A D/I mux allows part of a data stream to be dropped and inserted. D/I functions are being explored for ATM.
DA	Destination Address The Data Link and Network layers have addresses.
DAB	Dynamically Allocatable Bandwidth DAB allows a network to allocate bandwidth to specific applications as the application needs it. This is a concept rather than a technology; it is also known as bandwidth on demand. ATM and SMDS promise DAB.
DACS	Digital Access and Cross Connect Switching A DACS allows you to route T-1 lines and DS-0s within the T-1 to various outgoing T-1 ports. You can think of this as a large and sophisticated DS switching matrix.

dB	Decibel Decibels are a measure of the quality of the data signal compared to the noise level.
DCC	Digital Cross Connect A DCC is a generic DACS.
DCE	Data Circuit-terminating Equipment Data circuit-terminating equipment terminates a circuit in a data communications system. A DCE is a packet switch, a CSU, a modem, etc. See DTE.
DE	Discard Eligibility The DE bit in the frame relay frame indicates that this frame is in excess of the sender's CIR and can be dropped if congestion occurs.
Delay	If a frame does not arrive precisely when expected, SONET may need to buffer it, which will delay it. Minimizing transit delay is essential for voice traffic. Delay is a constant preoccupation for network managers making decisions about their networks, if the networks include voice, video, and some sensitive data protocols.
descriptors	Traffic descriptors One of a series of definitions of traffic that are part of the traffic contract. TTDs and STDs are (you continue):
DLCI	Data Link Connection Identifier The DLCI is the destination address in frame relay frames.
downstream	Toward the endpoints/users. Except in the case of:
DS-0	Digital Signal Level 0 A DS-0 is the basic digital channel, 64 Kbps for voice or data.

DS-1 Digital Signal Level 1

This is the digital signal level corresponding to T-1 service for North America. A DS-1 delivers 1.544 Mbps, of which 8 Kbps covers signaling and the rest is available for payload.

DS-2 Digital Signal Level 2

DS-2 is popular in Japan and is composed of 4 DS-1s, about 6 Mbps. It is called J-2.

DS-3 Digital Signal Level 3

The DS-3 level corresponds to T-3 service in North America or 44.8 Mbps.

DSAP Destination Service Access Point

The DSAP identifies the service at the destination layer that the sending layer must pass an SDU to. For example, when Layer 2 passes an SDU to Layer 3, it uses a particular DSAP between those 2 layers.

DSS1 D Channel Signaling System

Another name for Q.931(ISDN).

DSU Digital Service Unit

A DSU converts RS-232 data streams to a line coding compatible with the telco local loop. The DSU usually works in tandem with a CSU.

DTE Data Terminal Equipment

A DTE is a computer or other desktop RS-232 device that connects to a DCE in a packet switching network.

DXI Data Exchange Interface

In SMDS, DXI is the interface between the CP router and the DSU/CSU. It adds a header and trailer that is stripped by the CSU prior to sending the payload over SNI.

E.164 — ITU address scheme for ATM

E-1 — E-1 Service

E-1 is sometimes referred to as a European version of T-1 because it was developed by CEPT. Actually, E-1 is the digital signaling standard for the entire world outside of North America and Japan. The E-1 data rate equals 30 DS-0s, for an aggregate data rate of 2.048 Mbps.

EA — Extended Address

In frame relay, the extended address field allows you to specify a larger than average address. The LMI consortium has adopted this strategy, expanding the I.122 standard that calls for standard addresses only.

ELAN — Emulated LAN (LANE)

ATM interfaces to legacy LANs and emulates those LANs across the ATM backbone. Your definition:

EOC — Embedded Operations Channels

The EOC transmits network management in SONET. D1 through D3 octets in SOH and D4 through D12 in LOH are called EOCs when the telco is using them for management.

EPD

Your definition:

ESF — Extended Superframe

Extended Superframe is 24 bytes by 24 rows so it is equivalent to 24 standard frames. Every 193rd bit in the frame is the F (framing) bit. The payload equals 24 x 192 bits. The framing bits are C, D, F0 and F1. The C bits contain a CRC check sum while the D bits perform FDL. The F bits maintain synchronization.

ETSI — European Telecom Standards Institute

ETSI creates standards, then proposes to ISO and the ITU.

F, G, H

F	F Bit There are several types of F bits. The F bit in T-1 delimits a frame. It violates the line coding so it cannot be confused with data. Every 193rd bit in the T-1 frame is an F bit (framing). Other F bits repeat 8,000 times per second. The F bits delimit the Superframe and Extended Superframe.
FAD	Frame Relay Access Device A FAD (or FRAD) converts data traffic in some other format into frame relay format. It usually sits between a bridge or router and the frame relay network, since frame relay is frequently carrying LAN to LAN traffic.
FCC	Federal Communications Commission The FCC regulates many aspects of data communications and telecom in the US.
FCS	Frame Check Sequence The FCS is a generic concept. Most frame types have a check character or field at the end of the frame to allow the receiver to detect bit errors. FCSs are frequently CRCs.
FDDI	Fiber Distributed Data Interface ANSI developed FDDI as a 100 Mbps LAN standard for data. The FDDI protocols are now available on Cat. 5 UTP.
FEBE	Far End Block Errors The SONET receiver uses the Z2 octet to tell the sender a count of FEBEs on the incoming line. Z2 is in LOH. BIP8 is used to detect the errors.
FECN	Forward Explicit Congestion Notification FECN and BECN are extremely primitive congestion management facilities in the basic frame relay frame. LMI

will eventually provide much more robust facilities.

FERF — Far End Receiver Failure

In SONET, the PTE uses this signal to tell the sender that a failure occurred. This really refers to a path failure.

Float — Floating Mode in SONET

In floating mode, the payload is called a synchronous payload envelope because it does not have to start right after the overhead bytes. It can start anywhere in the payload part of the frame, a process called floating. Floating mode allows a mux to avoid buffering a frame that arrives slightly earlier or later than expected. The floating SPE may be part of a larger payload that itself is floating. See positive and negative stuffing and the SPE

flow — A label-swapping term in mixed ATM and IP-switched LANs. Your definition:

FOTS — Fiber Optic Transmission Systems

Any system that uses fiber optic media and the appropriate switches. This can include SONET.

FR — Frame Relay

Frame relay is a Data Link service specified in I.122. It is designed for high-speed wide-area transport of data. See DLCI. Some analysts believe that ATM will remove the need for frame relay but ATM is not the perfect solution for all applications.

FRAD — Frame Relay Access Device

A FRAD takes LAN traffic and transforms it into frame relay frames. Same as FAD.

Frame — Frame has many meanings, depending on the context. As a noun, it usually means a Data Link entity: an Ethernet frame, etc. As a verb, see Framing.

Framing — Framing is a universal requirement in serial data communi-

	cations, the essential division of a data stream into fields with specific meanings. The second and different meaning of the word framing is the bits and octets that sender and receiver use to pass control information, do diagnosis and management and keep their clocks synchronized. Both T-1/T-3 and SONET, since they are physical fabric switching technologies, refer to this type of framing.
FT1	Fractional T-1
	For companies who do not need full T-1 capacity, carriers offer multiple DS-0s, known as fractional T-1.
full-duplex	A type of network switch or NIC that: (you continue)
G	G bytes in SONET
	The G bytes are located in POH and handle error management including4 bits of FEBE.
G.708	SONET to SDH conversion
	This standard defines SDH and indirectly describes how STM1 maps to OC3.
Gbps	Gigabits Per Second
	1,000 Mbps.
GCAC	
	Your definition:
GCRA	
	Your definition:
GFC	Generic Flow Control
	GFC is the first 4 bits of the UNI ATM cell header.
Group	VT Groups
	VTs are put into VT groups arranged in 12 columns. Each

	group can only carry a single type of VT. Seven groups can be multiplexed into the SPE of OC1.
H	H1, H2, H3, H4 octets The H1, H2 and H3 octets are part of the line overhead of an STS frame. H1 and H2 point to the start of the payload in floating mode. The payload could contain ATM cells. H3 is usually null, unless it is being used for a negative stuff byte when the payload is early by = 1 byte. H4 is part of path overhead and it specifies which channel's signaling bits are in the current VT. See also S bits.
HEC	Header Error Control HEC is the last octet of the ATM cell header. HEC is a header error check sequence.
HSSI	High Speed Serial Interface HSSI is a new high-speed interface that can carry data up to 1.2 Gbps. HSSI interfaces exist to SONET, DS3, frame relay, ISDN, etc.
hub	You define:

I, J, K, L

I	I bits in SONET If a frame needs to shift forward one octet and use the positive stuff byte, in H4, the sender alerts the receiver to this shift by inverting the I bits in the H pointers.
I	I Standards The ITU/TSS includes ISDN, B-ISDN, ATM, frame relay and other technologies in this family.
IAB	Internet Activities Board The IAB determines policy for the Internet.

ICI	InterExchange Carrier Interface ICI defines the interface between local telco switches and the IEC switch in SMDS.
IEC	InterExchange Carrier An IEC carries traffic between LATAs, either across the state or across the country. Since the Telecom Act of 1996, the local area is open to IEC competition in the USA.
IEEE	Institute for Electrical and Electronics Engineers The IEEE is a professional organization that has developed many LAN standards in the 802 family.
IETF	Internet Engineering Task Force The IETF makes technical decisions concerning the Internet.
IFC	Your definition:
IP	Internet Protocol Network Layer of the Internet Protocol Stack
I-PNNI	Integrated Private Network-Network Interface A routing protocol for mixed ATM networks, which:
ISDN	Integrated Services Digital Network ISDN is currently the rage for telecommuting and access to the Internet. See also SS7.
ISO	International Organization for Standardization ISO developed the OSI model and hundreds of vitally important communications standards. No, it's not a typo, that's really what the acronym means. ISO is a voluntary international standards organization that cooperates closely with the ITU. ANSI is the US delegate to ISO.

isochronous	Traffic types for which precise timing relations are important, for example, realtime voice and video.
ISSI	Inter Switching Systems Interface ISSI in SMDS defines the interface between different switching systems in a carrier network, either different vendors or related but not identical technologies.
ISUP	Integrated Services Digital Network User Part Also known as ISDN-UP, this is a collection of signaling protocols for SS7 in the Q.7xx series. In ISDN terminology, a User Part is a CPE responsibility.
ITU	International Telecommunications Union The ITU is part of the United Nations. The TSS and a related radio standards organization (the RSS) report to the ITU.
J	J Character In FDDI, J and K are non-data characters, used as delimiters.
J1	SONET J1 Octet The J1 octet is the first octet in the SPE. In floating mode, the J1 octet moves to the left or the right by 1 column in the STS frame. The H1 and H2 pointer octets of the previous frame point to the starting location of the next frame's SPE, namely the J1.
J-2	See DS-2.
K	K bytes in SONET The K bytes are in LOH and control automatic protection switching for the line.
label	You define:
LANE	LAN Emulation An ATM Forum standard that allows ATM/Ethenet connec-

tion. See LES, LECS, BUS. Your notes:

LAP — Link Access Protocol

There are many LAP variants used as data link protocols: D for the ISDN D channels; M for modems; B in OSI networks. LAP-B is almost identical to HDLC.

leaky bucket — A form of GCRA

Your definition:

LEC — Local Exchange Carrier

Your local telco, offering service within a LATA. Your LEC cannot carry your traffic beyond the LATA border.

LECS — LAN EMulation & Configuration Server

A LANE component that (you continue):

LED — Light Emitting Diode

The light source in relatively low speed optical fiber technology, like fiber Ethernet. Higher speed systems use lasers.

LEN — Local Exchange Node

A fancy term for a switch at your local CO.

LES — LAN Emulation Server

The LANE component that (you continue):

LLC — Logical Link Control

IEEE 802.2.

LMI — Link Management Interface

The management standard for frame relay.

LOC — Loss of Cell Delineation

LOC occurs when the receiver sees 7 consecutive HEC errors in ATM.

locked — Locked mode SPE

In locked mode STS-1, the J1 data octet which is the beginning of SPE occurs immediately following the 3 overhead octets. See floating mode.

LOF — Loss of Frame

The mux has been unable to find framing bits for a few seconds and gives up on the frame.

LOH — Line Overhead

In the STS overhead, 6 rows by 3 columns of LOH follows the SOH. LOH is created and managed by LTEs. FEBE, the H1-H3 pointers and BIP8 octets are all included in LOH.

LOP — Loss of Pointer

In SONET, the mux can't find the pointer octets. If it's floating point, you've lost the data as well.

LSB — Least Significant Bit

The LSB in an octet is the bit with the lowest place value. Some protocols transmit addresses with LSBs first while others transmit MSBs first.

LTE — Line Terminating Equipment

The LTE terminates a SONET line and processes the LOH. The LTE creates the SPE and places it in either locked or floating mode in the frame.

M

MAC	Medium Access Control Lower half of the Data Link Layer, defines frame format, access control, addresses and error detection.
MARS	Multicast Address Resolution Server Resolves ATM to Ethernet addresses. And:
MBS	Maximum Burst Size Your definition:
MCF	MAC Convergence Function This is an SMDS term for the interface from 802.2 LLC to the MAC Sublayer. The MAC convergence protocol (MCP) accomplishes this function
MCR	Mean Cell Rate Your definition:
MDF	Main Distribution Frame The MDF is where the main trunks coming in from the telco are punched down and brought into the building. The MDF feeds IDFs.
MF	Multi-Frame The MF field of SDH signals that a VT is carrying multiple frames—E1 superframes, for example.
MFA	Multi-Frame Alignment See MF. Also E1 has an MFA signal in slot 16 (its framing slot) to indicate that it is part of a superframe.

MID — Message IDentifier (SMDS)

The MID is put into all the L2PDUs that were created from a specific L3PDU (packet). When the L2PDUs are received and put back together again, the L3PDU can be recreated. The L2PDU lists the MID in header and trailer.

MPOA — Multiprotocol Over ATM

An ATM Forum standard that interfaces ATM to IP and (you continue):

MSB — Most Significant Bit

The opposite of LSB.

N, O, P

NATA	North American Telecommunications Association An important telecom trade organization, NATA has been encouraging the development of SONET products.
NDF	New Data Flag If the SPE has slipped by more than 1 octet, you cannot use H3 for stuffing. H1 and H2 change to indicate NDF and point to the new SPE position in SONET.
NHRP	Next Hop Resolution Protocol A routing protocol for mixed ATM networks. Your notes:
NI	Network Interface The demark point between the customer premises and the local CO or LEC's POP.
nibble	Half a byte 4 bits. GFC in ATM is 1 nibble long.
NIST	National Institute for Standards and Technology NIST encourages technical standards in the US.
NNI	Network to Network Interface In ATM, NNI defines the interface between 2 switches. Developed by the ATM Forum.
NRZ	Non Return to Zero Most modern coding schemes are of this type, where the signal does not have to transition to zero, but can pass through zero.
NRZI	Non Return to Zero Invert on 1 The signal transitions from one polarity to the other to indicate a 1 value and remains unchanged for 0. Another name for this is AMI, used in T-1.

NT-1x	Network Termination, type 1 and Type 2 In ISDN, the device that holds the U interface is usually the NT-1 because it is the first device on CP that interfaces with the CO. The NT-2 interfaces with the NT-1 on one side and with (usually) LAN devices on the other.
NTN	Network Terminal Number Part of the X.121 global addressing standard, the NTN identifies a particular device. ISDN uses X.121.
OAM	Operation and Maintenance In SONET, this includes all overhead and maintenance.
OC-1	Optical Carrier, Level 1 The optical carrier level is how you specify the speed of a SONET pipe. If you want to specify the framing formats, you specify the STS level. OC-1 corresponds to STS-1 at 51.84 Mbps.
Octet	8 bits This is a ITU/TSS term that means 8 bits. The term byte could potentially mean a character whose length is not exactly 8 bits and international standards require exactitude.
OOB	Out of Band With OOB signaling, like in ISDN, no potential user data bandwidth is being robbed to provide signaling bandwidth. T-carrier, where signaling is in-band, must rob bits for framing and signaling.
OOF	Out of Frame The OOF condition occurs when a mux can't delineate a frame in the bit stream; it can't find the framing bits.
OSI	Open Systems Interconnection OSI is a 7 layer model of network function.
PAD	Packet Assembler/Disassembler A PAD takes a local data stream and puts it into a specific wide area packet format. Many PAD types exist.

Path	SONET Path The Path is the entire connection from the sending user's premises (mux) to the receiver's premises. See POH.
PCM	Pulse Code Modulation PCM is the standard way to digitally encode voice on 64 Kbps DS-0s.
PCR	Peak Cell Rate Your definition:
PDH	Pleisiochronous digital hierarchy In North America, PDH gets you from your T-1 up to your T-3. It means "changing clocks".
PDS	Premises Distribution System This is the voice and data wiring on the customer premises.
PDU	Protocol Data Unit Each layer of the OSI model receives data units from the layers immediately above and below it. The entity that a layer processes (adds or deletes header.
Period	Frame period In STS-1, just like in T-1, the frame period or duration is 125 microseconds. The frame duration at higher STS levels is longer.
PING	Packet Internet Groper Used in the Internet, to see if a device is able to receive packets. Also used as a verb, in lowercase.
PIN	Personal ID Number Used with the ATMs that give you cash!
PLCP	Physical Layer Convergence Protocol The PLCP is the upper sublayer of the PHY, above the PMD. The PLCP defines how the essential framing formats

	of the transmission map to the MAC above it. SONET has a PLCP to connect to ATM, and other frame layer technologies.
plenum	A wiring designation It means that the wire can be used without being placed in conduit. It conforms to fire codes because it is specially coated and will not give off toxic fumes when it burns.
PMD	Physical Medium Dependent The PMD sublayer of the Physical Layer interfaces directly with the physical medium and performs the most basic bit transmission functions in the network.
PNNI	Private/Public Network-Network Interface Your definition:
POH	Path Overhead The first POH octet occurs either in byte position 4 of the STS frame (in locked mode) or anywhere in the frame in floating mode. The first POH octet starts the SPE. Subsequent POH octets are placed in position immediately below it.
POP	Point of Presence A carrier or provider has a point of presence that you can make a dialup or leased connection to. A carrier can have FRADs at many locations in a metropolitan area and then a high-speed trunk that collects the low-speed data streams.
PPP	Point-to-Point Protocol PPP is a wide-area, high-speed protocol for IP networks.
pps	packets per second Performance measures on routers, switches, etc.is generally measured in packets per second.
PRA	Primary Rate Access PRA is the service designation for PRI. See also BRA.

PRC	Primary Reference Clock This is the clock used as a stratum 1 clocking source. This clock is the master clock in your SONET network.
PRI	Primary Rate Interface The primary rate interface in ISDN is 23B+D in North America and Japan, and 30B+D everywhere else. This difference in how PRI is defined parallels the difference between T-1 and E-1. PRI was designed for serious business access. The D channel is 64 Kbps. See BRI.
PRS	Primary Rate Source A stratum 1 clock. See PRC.
PSE	Packet Switching Exchange A packet switching exchange accepts incoming packet data flows and processes them: multiplexing, switching, etc. This is a generic term used in discussions of ATM.
PSN	Packet Switched Network A network using packet switching, as opposed to circuit or cell switching. PSNs are WANs dedicated to data traffic.
PT	Payload Type See PTI.
PTE	Path Terminating Equipment A PTE terminates the path in a SONET network. The PTE reads the path overhead bits, performs error control and allows separate management of each individual path. The path overhead (POH) defines the SPE.
PTI	Payload Type Identifier The PTI defines what type of payload the information field includes: data or network operations, and whether the cell experienced congestion along the path. PTI is a 3 bit field in the ATM cell header, followed by CLP.
PTT	Post, Telegraph and Telephone Around the world (except for the US), government ministries, called PTTs, regulate all communications

matters within their respective countries: determine what equipment may be manufactured or imported, what may be connected to the local telco system, and require adherence to ITU/TSS standards.

PUC — Public Utility Commission

In the US, individual states regulate utilities, including communications utilities, within their borders. PUCs cannot regulate interstate commerce.

PVC — Permanent Virtual Circuit

Frame relay at present is primarily a PVC phenomenon. A PVC links two geographical sites and is provisioned by the provider. DLCIs are basically PVCs. A virtual circuit mimics a physical circuit except that bandwidth is not physically (only logically) allocated to the sender and receiver.

Q, R

Q — Q-Series Standards

In the ITU/TSS, Q.x standardizes signaling.The ATM Forum is developing recommendations to ensure that development of ATM products follows B-ISDN/ISDN signaling standards, to prevent incompatibilities.

QFC — Quantum Flow Control

Which (you add):

QOS — Quality Of Service

QOS specifies the performance requirements of the network delivery mechanism. It measures: (you add)

R	R Interface in ISDN The R interface (reference point) connects a non-ISDN device to a TA.
RACE	Research For Advanced Communications In Europe This is a vendor consortium developing broadband networking solutions in Europe.
Rate	Line transmission capacity A line rate is the maximum Mbps that the transmission line can pass between two points.
rate-based	A form of ATM ABR congestion management that (you add):
repeater	You define:
RM	Resource Management (cell) Your definition:
RTS	Residual Time Stamp The RTS is carried in the SAR-PDU. The time stamp allows the ATM switch that reassembles cells into their original frames to reassemble them correctly.
RZ	Return to Zero RZ line coding standards request that the signal pause at 0 voltage when the signal crosses from positive to negative.High-speed networking uses NRZ for efficiency.

S, T, U

S	S bit in VT1.5 Each S octet in the floating VT1.5 includes C bits for

control and S bits for stuffing. See S octet, VT, float.

S — S octet in SONET

If you want to put a T-1 into a VT, the payload will have only 24 octets because you need 3 octets of overhead. Two of the octets point to the payload in floating mode and the third octet is reserved for signaling and stuffing (the S octet). Part of this octet are the ABCD signaling bits and another bit is an F bit. If the VT carries an ESF, part of the F bits are FDLs.

SA — Source Address

The SA and DA are in the MAC header and the IP header.

SAP — Service Access Point

You access the services of a particular layer through a SAP and each layer has a DSAP and SSAP.The Physical Layer process sends the service data unit (SDU) through its DSAP to the Data Link Layer.

SAR — Segmentation and Reassembly

The SAR sublayer in ATM takes the streams passed on by the AALs, segments into cells and passes them to the ATM Layer for switching. On the other side, SAR takes the cells and reassembles them back into frames, circuits, etc.

SAR-PDU — SAR Protocol Data Unit

You add the 5 octet ATM header to the 48 octet SAR-PDU to create a complete ATM cell.

SCCP — Signaling Connection Control Part

SCCP controls connection maintenance in SS7.

SCP — Service Control Point

The SCP supports special carrier services like ANI and resides in a telco central office. It is part of SS7.

SCR — Sustained Cell Rate

Your definition:

SDF — Subdistribution Frame

If your premises wiring is structured, you bring your wiring from the main distribution frame (MDF) to intermediate distribution frames (IDF) to subdistribution frames (SDF) which are the last wiring termination points before the wiring fans out into wall connections for the users.

SDH — Synchronous Digital Hierarchy

CEPT created SDH, which has been accepted as a standard everywhere except in SONET-land, which is North America. SDH transport begins with synchronous transport module (STM-1) at 155.52 Mbps. Subrates on SDH are multiples of E-carrier, not T-carrier. At STM-1 and higher, SONET and SDH are mostly compatible.

SDU — Service Data Unit

An SDU is passed through a SAP. If you call it a PDU instead, no one will hate you.

SES — Severely Errored Second

Any 1 second of time, in which the BER is more than 1 per thousand, there are more than 319 CRC errors in the extended superframe, the frame has slipped or there is an alarm.

SF — Superframe

Twelve T-1 frames.

SI — Sequenced Information

This is a LAP-D frame that carries user information.

SIP — SMDS Interface Protocol

SIP has 3 layers of function, including convergence with ATM.

SIPO Signaling Indication Processor Outage

SIPO is the alarm that is generated when the processor that sends and receives signaling packets fails. In SS 7, a signaling packet is called an indication.

SIR Sustained Information Rate

The SIR is the average throughput that a sender expects to present to an SMDS network.

SMDS Switched Multimegabit Data Service

SMDS is a Data Link Layer service that can be implemented above SONET, T- or E-carrier. It was designed for data.

SNA SDH Network Aspects

Standards for VC payloads and payload management in SDH. (I'll bet you thought this had something to do with IBM.)

SNAP Subnetwork Access Protocol

SNAP adds an additional subnetwork address in the LLC header, to allow specific subnets to be addressed.

SNI Subscriber Network Interface

SNI is the point where the public ATM/SMDS network reaches the customer premises. This is the most important interface and the one receiving the most development work at this time.

SNMP Simple Network Management Protocol

SNMP was developed for the TCP/IP protocol stack and has evolved into the most important network management protocol available today. Eventually, network managers would like to use a relative of SNMP to manage their ATM nodes as well.

SOH Section Overhead

Section overhead manages connections and errors between major multiplexing elements. SOH follows line overhead in the transport overhead section of an STS frame.

SONET	Synchronous Optical Network SONET is a North American high-speed synchronous network designed to run on optical fiber. SDH is used outside of North America.
SPE	Synchronous Payload Envelope The SPE is the actual payload being transported in SONET, plus path overhead (POH).
SS7	Signaling System 7 SS7 is out-of-band signaling for ISDN and will eventually replace common channel signaling (CCS6). SS7 is the wide-area continuation of the local D channel.
SSAP	Source Service Access Point See SAP.
SSCS	Service-Specific Convergence Sublayer The SSCS, the upper sublayer of the CS in ATM, handles error recovery. The lower layer (CPCS) detects errors. The specifics of error recovery depend on the AAL type.
SSM	Single Segment Message A frame that comes through the AAL from a higher level protocol and is so small that it can fit into a single ATM payload.
STD	Source Traffic Descriptors, see descriptors
STE	Section Terminating Equipment The section is the connection between 2 repeaters, so it is the lowest level of SONET overhead.
STM	Synchronous Transport Module SDH transport levels, starting at OC-3.
store-and-forward	A type of switch that (you continue):

stratum	Clock classification Stratum means "level" in Latin. A stratum 1 clock is a master clock that will drift no more than 10^{11} with respect to another stratum 1 clock. Other components in your network may use lower stratum (2+) clocks whose tolerances are less rigorous. Most SONET switches use stratum 1 clocks.
STS-1	Synchronous Transport Signal Level 1 The STS levels are equivalent to OC levels in SONET.
stuff	Stuff byte H3 byte in SONET, OC-1. Used by floating mode.
SU	Segmentation Unit The SU is the payload of the L2PDU in SMDS.
subframe	Smaller than a frame A VT is an example of subframe framing in SONET. The unit of transfer is smaller than an SPE.
subrate	Less than the expected rate If the incoming stream is less than the expected line rate, the bits must be put into a VT or VC and carried as subrate transport. To subrate a T-1 trunk means to divide it into DS-0s.
switch	You define:
T1	ANSI committee T1E1 is the SNI committee and T1X1 handles SONET.
T-1	T-carrier, level 1 1.544 mbps

TA — Terminal Adapter

A TA converts a non-ISDN device to ISDN compatible.

TOH — Transport Overhead

TOH is SOH plus LOH in SONET. It is found in the first 3 octets of the 90 octet frame format.

traffic contract — The agreement between the endpoint or edge device and the ATM network. And (you add):

traffic descriptors

see descriptors

TSI — Time Slot Interchange

A TSI process buffers the contents of a timeslot in a TDM so that the outgoing stream is in a different order than the incoming stream.

TSS — Telecom Standards Sector, see ITU

TTD — Transit Traffic Descriptors, see descriptors

TU — Tributary Unit

A TU is conceptually similar to a VT, only in SDH. A TU is a virtual container (VC) plus the H3 pointers. In SDH the pointers are part of the TU, not part of TOH like they are in SONET. See also SDH and AU.

TUG — TU Group

SDH defines specific TUGs.

Type — Classification of repeater

And (you continue):

U — Universal Interface

Universal interface between CO and CP in standard ISDN.

UA	Unnumbered Acknowledgment An LLC frame that accepts connection requests (802.2)
UBR	Unassigned Bit Rate Your definition:
ULSI	Ultra Large Scale Integration In order to implement high-speed technologies at the chip level (hardware always executes faster than software) we need ULSI.
UNI	User to Network Interface The UNI is the demark point of ATM at the customer premises. UNI cells include a 4 bit GFC field. UNI standards are created by the ATM Forum.
UNR	Uncontrolled Not Ready This is the signaling bit for T-1 in Japan.
upstream	Toward the backbone. And (you continue):
UPC	Usage Parameter Control Your definition:
USP	Usage Sensitive Pricing You have bandwidth on demand and pay only for the packets or cells you present to the network. In present implementations, you generally need to oversubscribe to make sure you have enough bandwidth for your peak usage times.
UTC	Universal Time, Coordinated Since SONET is synchronous, maintaining synchronized clocks is of critical importance. UTC keeps clocks coordinated.

UTP — Unshielded Twisted Pair

ATM on UTP needs to be Cat. 5.

V

VBR-rt — Variable Bit Rate, realtime

Your definition:

VBR-nrt — Variable Bit Rate, non-realtime

Your definition:

VC — Virtual Circuit

This software entity guarantees packet sequencing and message integrity. In most LANs, this is a Transport Layer software entity like TCP or SPX. VCs are also known as connection oriented network service (CONS). ATM creates VCs at the Data Link layer.

VC — Virtual Container

This is the ITU/TSS version of a Virtual Tributary (VT), in SDH. The container allows you to put a slower channel into a higher speed SDH channel.

VCC — Virtual Channel Connection

These VCCs can be grouped in VPCs. Each VCC has traffic descriptors associated with it and (you continue):

VCI — Virtual Channel Identifier

Your definition:

VF — Voice Frequency

The frequency range for human voice is 300–3300 Hz.

VG	Voice Grade wire This is Cat. 3 UTP.
virtual source or destination	Endpoint of a congestion loop And: (you add)
VLAN	Virtual LAN A logical LAN, that you configure in software rather than moving plugs at the patch panel.
VLSI	Very Large Scale Integration SONET chips use VLSI.
VP	Virtual Path See VPI.
VPC	Virtual Path Connection A virtual path connection is a collection of VCCs. The ATM Layer handles VPC creation.
VPI	Virtual Path Identifier The virtual path identifier is one of the fields in the ATM header. It specifies the VP/VPC carried in the cell payload.
VT	Virtual Tributary The virtual tributary is a slower speed stream (T-1, for example) encapsulated inside a SONET payload.
VTE	Virtual Tributary Envelope The VTE falls within the SONET synchronous payload envelope (SPE)

W, X, Y, Z

X	X Series Standards The ITU/TSS designates most data communications standards in the X.xx family. The high speed networking technologies are all in the I family, for ISDN
z	802.3z, the Gigabit Ethernet subcommittee/working group
Z	Z byte in SONET The Z bytes carry the line FEBE.
ZBTSI	Zero Byte Time Slot Interchange In order to maintain proper clocking on T-1 lines, it's necessary for the transmitter to stuff 1s whenever there are too many 0s in a series. We say that ZBTSI and other techniques are needed to maintain the 1s density for clocking. This process of adding 1s is called bit stuffing. See B8ZS.

About The Authors

V.C. Marney-Petix develops and delivers both live and computer-based training programs on network technology and management through Marpet University and delivers consulting services through Marpet Technical Services. Her course list includes specific technologies as well as network redesign workshops in which attendees get free consulting on their network problems. She regularly travels to teach in South America, Asia and even (gasp!) the East Coast. When not working, she pays attention to her incredibly talented and well-trained house rabbits and cats, dances in costume at Victorian, Regency and English Country music events and gardens madly, with medleys of mulching and harvesting. You may contact the author directly at:

Marpet University
PO Box 2275, Fremont, CA 94536
(510) 792-9204, ext. 2 or email at **marpetu@home.com**

Sandrella Salins

Sandrella Salins has been a trainer, training manager, marketing manager and international division manager for 15 years. She has worked with technical, sales, marketing and support audiences, providing clear and succinct presentations on tough topics, from ATM to Executive Negotiating Skills and Multicultural Communication. Most recently, she has been working with health care organizations and with the networking industry. She lives and works in southern California, but works extensively with Northern California companies and international clients. Sandrella is International Marketing Manager of Numidia Press and has also worked as International Training manager at Apple, Marpet University and several international companies.Sandrella has been advanced to candidacy in the Ph.D. program in Clinical Psychology and speaks 4 languages fluently.

If you have comments on this book, please communicate with us (rather than the authors) at **Numidia Press**. We appreciate your feedback!

Numidia Press • P.O. Box 2281 • Fremont, CA 94536

Phone (510) 790-1199 • Fax (510) 797-5053, numidia@aol.com

Comments

Title: *Gigabit Ethernet*

Where did you acquire this book?

❐ mail order

❐ bookstore/online (name) ______________________________

❐ employer (name) ____________________________________

❐ training course ______________________________________

I'd like you to know that: (tell us where we goofed, did a great job, could make improvements, left something out, etc.)

____

____

____

Tell us about yourself. Your name/address/phone is useful if we don't understand and need to call you to clarify, but you can remain incognito if you prefer. Your job title or function will help us to understand what kind of reader the problem impacts and this is important to us. An industry is equally helpful.

____

____

____

We appreciate all your help in making the next edition of this book even better than the present one. Thank you!

Numidia Press • P.O. Box 2281 • Fremont, CA 94536
Phone (510) 790-1199 • Fax (510) 797-5053

Order Form

Please send me the books in the Self-Paced Learning Series:

________copies of *GEnet/ATM &High-Speed Networks(* **$45.95)**

________copies of *Integrating ATM* **($39.95)**

________copies of *Bridges, Routers, Gateways! (* **$35.95)**

_________ copies of *Mastering Network Management* (**$29.95**)

_________ copies of *LANs! LANs! LANs!* (**$35.95**)

_________ copies of the Glossary (Mac or PC, pls circle which) $80

$________ Subtotal (**Don't forget your discounts!**)

$________ CA addresses add 8.25% sales tax

$________ Shipping ($3 for 1st book, $1.50 each additional book.)

(US domestic shipments only. Non-US addresses cost more.)

$________ Amount enclosed

Name ____

Company/Title ______________________________________

Address ____

City ________________________ State _______ Zip ___________

Full money-back guarantee!

Please make check payable to:

Numidia Press
P.O. Box 2281
Fremont, CA 94536
(510) 790-1199

Fax (510) 797-5053

Discount Schedule

2-10 20% off

11-30 30% off

31-50 40% off

Call for larger quantities

numidia@aol.com (orders) or marpetu@home.com (authors)

or call toll-free 800-356-9315

http//www.best.com/~numidia

Coupon

For only $100 (or see coupon below), you can get a disk version of the High-Speed LAN/WAN Glossary. Put it on your PC, Mac or even server. Your site license allows you unlimited copying on your site and at your home or laptop. Other sites of your company, your buddies at other companies, your spouse, mother-in-law, etc. require additional licenses or you are eligible to be visited by our team of unforgiving, humorless lawyers. Talk to us before doing anything questionable. We can always develop a custom license to cover multiple sites and special situations.

Coupon

This coupon and $80 gives you a disk version (Windows or Mac) of the High-Speed LAN/WAN Glossary.

Good until February 28, 1998

The Numidia Catalog of Stars

Bridges, Routers, Gateways!, 2nd Edition

Your comprehensive introduction to bridges, switches, routers and gateways, for LANs, WANs and combination networks. Continue your study of LAN/WANs! Second Edition available in 1998.

V. C. Marney-Petix $35.95

Mastering Network Management

Your comprehensive tutorial and reference on all five essential areas of management: fault, configuration, performance, accounting and security. Two complete chapters on SNMP and the manager/agent model, plus chapters on organizational and fiscal issues.

ISBN: 1-880548-13-5 220 pages $29.95

Valerie Swisher, David Harris and V. C. Marney-Petix

LANs! LANs! LANs!, 2nd Edition

LANs! LANs! LANs! (1996 edition) is a comprehensive look at local area networks. You get a detailed chapter on network operating systems (including Windows NT), client/server networking and middleware and an in-depth introduction to network management. You learn the latest in high speed LAN options as well as switching hubs. 2nd edition available in 1998 .

ISBN: 1-880548-39-9 230 pages $35.95

V. C. Marney-Petix

New for 1997!

Cool Software for Kids and Adults!

• **Flying Numbers** is a teaching game for kids of all ages to learn to add and subtract, in English, Spanish and Russian. Adults can learn a new language, and play the more challenging levels. Runs on Windows, including W95. $250 site license for groups.

• **Applications Training CBTs** for all popular PC programs, in Spanish. All the common Microsoft/industry applications. $500-800.

• **High-Speed LAN/WAN Glossary,** $100 w/out coupon, $80 with coupon. Site license, Mac and PC/Windows versions.

This is it — your site license for a comprehensive lookup on all high-speed LAN/WAN terms. Copy as often as you like for internal use.

New for 1998!

Integrating ATM With Legacy LANs

Everything you need to know, in as much detail as you can stand, about connecting ATM to existing Ethernet and IP networks. We explore LANE, MPOA, Layer3 switching, IP switching, tag and label switching and more.

Sandrella Salins and V. C. Marney-Petix, 220 pp. $45.95, includes an ATM integration glossary.

More Numidia Resources

- Love the Internet? You can order by sending email to **numidia@aol.com**
- Love your Numidia Press book? Tell us about it! If you give us permission to use your comments in our promotions, we will send you a free book or audiotape and arrange for you to have lunch with one of our authors.
- International buyers in the Asia/Pacific area please contact Technologica Pty. Ltd., 48 Hamilton Street, Lane Cove 2066, Sydney, Australia. In India, contact the Institute of Telecom Management, 824 Deccan Gymkhana, Pune 411 004 India.
- Subscribe to **Network News & Views** (NNV) for latest industry product news and commentary on industry trends, as well as special-price offers. Just send an email or quick note to the NNV department.
- Call our 800# with your credit card. 800–356–9315

Index